MERCY IN THE CITY

MERCY IN THE CITY

How to Feed the Hungry,
Give Drink to the Thirsty,
Visit the Imprisoned, and
Keep Your Day Job

KERRY WEBER

LOYOLA PRESS.
A JESUIT MINISTRY
Chicago

LOYOLA PRESS.
A JESUIT MINISTRY

3441 N. Ashland Avenue
Chicago, Illinois 60657
(800) 621-1008
www.loyolapress.com

Scripture quotations are from *New Revised Standard Version Bible: Catholic Edition*, copyright © 1989, 1993 National Council of the Churches of Christ in the United States of America. Used by permission. All rights reserved.

Parts of chapters 20 and 21 contain excerpts based on an article that first appeared in *America* magazine: "Theology Behind Bars: A Jesuit chaplain bring St. Ignatius to San Quentin," by Kerry Weber, July 2, 2012. Chapters 13 and 22 contain excerpts based on an interview given to the National Catholic Reporter: "America associate editor sees hope for fractured church," by Sr. Camille D'Arienzo, March 20, 2012.

Cover art credits: texture, Ratana21/Shutterstock.com, illustration, Lavandaart/ Shutterstock.com.

Back cover author photo credit: David Chen.

ISBN-13: 978-0-8294-3892-5
ISBN-10: 0-8294-3892-0
Library of Congress Control Number: 2013953837

Printed in the United States of America.

18 19 20 21 22 23 24 25 26 Bang 14 13 12 11 10 9 8 7 6

For Marian Elizabeth Begley

CONTENTS

And the ministers of the church must be ministers of mercy above all.
—Pope Francis, *America*

INTRODUCTION

I sit on my bed, lace up my shoes, and assure myself that if the nuns reject me on the basis of my footwear, I don't want anything to do with them anyway. After sifting through my closet, I decide to wear dark jeans and a black sweater with a white collar sewn into the neckline, so that it looks like I'm wearing a button-down shirt. This decision has come largely by default, as this item of clothing is more professional-looking than 98 percent of my wardrobe, which I've purchased mostly at thrift shops. However, the shoes I'm lacing up are new. And yet I'm still unsure if they are appropriate—white faux leather, with black stripes on the sides. They would be professional-looking if I were a professional bowler, or perhaps a golfer, but I am neither. In fact, I am not feeling particularly ready to be a professional anything. I am a college senior about to graduate. I am an English major without a specific career plan (which is to say, I am an English major). I am going on my first job interview, and I am searching for some feeling of control. So I decide I am going to wear whatever shoes I damn well please.

The interview is a couple of miles from campus, so I climb into the 1993 Camry I share with my younger brother, Matthew. A few minutes later I pull up in front of a white, multifamily house with a small front porch. Sister Carol Mary, a Sister of Mercy with a long, dark ponytail, lets me in. I am immediately charmed by the eclectic nature of the furniture and religious imagery scattered about the house. A meal is being prepared by another Sister of Mercy along with a few other women, one of whom wears a sweatshirt with a nature scene on it. They are reheating leftovers from a recent Easter dinner. Mixed vegetables sit in a glass dish beside slices of baked ham and crusty bread.

As an interviewer for the Mercy Volunteer Corps, Sister Carol Mary is my first contact with the Mercy sisters' full-time volunteer program. If all goes well, when I leave the house, I will be one step closer to joining a community of fellow volunteers who have a desire to serve others—to "give back," as I and countless others, I'm sure, have said in our applications. Although I, for one, am not quite certain what I'm giving and to whom.

I'd spent hours flipping through a cross-referenced guide to domestic and international volunteer programs, as well as various brochures and pamphlets I'd picked up at my school's volunteer fair. Then I'd opened a simple brochure printed on bright yellow paper. Among the sites listed, one caught my eye: a group of volunteers would live in trailers on the Navajo reservation in the high desert of Arizona, it said. They would work at a school for children with special needs. I was struck by this description, because although everything in it would be new to me, it still felt like a place that was familiar, somewhere I could belong. And somehow this feeling had led me to this two-family house and this dinner and this interview, where I sat trying to convince a sister from a religious order I'd never heard of to let me join a bunch of people I'd never met so that I could travel to a place I'd never been and try to do a job for which I wasn't sure I was even qualified.

I sit down at the table, and we say grace together. The food is warm and comforting, and later in the evening the women clean up the table and I am led to the living room for an interview. As I walk out, one of the women, the one in the sweatshirt with the nature scene, looks at me and wishes me good luck. And then she looks down at my feet, and she says with genuine enthusiasm: I like your shoes. For the first time that evening, for the first time in a long time, I really feel like everything is going to be OK.

This was my first prayerful encounter with the charism, or animating spirit, of mercy. I certainly didn't realize then the impact the charism eventually would have on my life, how it would begin to settle into my consciousness during my time on the Navajo reservation, how it would motivate me even before I could explain what it meant. Or how years later, after moving to New York, it would push me to seek out the Sisters of Mercy and that spirit again. How, in a city with twenty-four-hour stores, eight million people, and infinite possibilities, it would help me find peace.

CHAPTER 1

—IN WHICH I HOST THE THIRD ANNUAL SUNNYSIDE PANCAKE DAY SPECTACULAR

At one point during the night, the contents of my refrigerator consist almost entirely of beer, wine, and a bag of baby carrots. I stare at the bottles illuminated by the tiny lightbulb and begin to wonder if I'm doing the right thing. "I need to get rid of this before tomorrow," I say to the crowd in the kitchen. "Drink up."

My apartment is warm and crowded with people, laughter, and the smell of pancakes, which slowly turn from a mushy beige to a fluffy toffee color on the electric griddle set in the middle of the kitchen table. I take a sip of beer.

It is early evening in mid-February, and I am in the midst of my annual, Tuesday-night pre-Lent party. The day is known to most Americans as Mardi Gras, but while rambling through a Wikipedia search a few years back, I had learned about the Irish and English custom of making pancakes on this day. It is said to have originated in the Middle Ages as a way to rid the house of some of the rich ingredients—milk, butter, eggs—before the rigid Lenten fasting began. I added a hyperlink to the e-mail invite, and thus the Annual Sunnyside Pancake Day Spectacular was born.

As most people are aware, Mardi Gras often involves overindulgence. The aim of my party is to help facilitate this excessive intake of food and (relatively responsible intake of) drink. I pledged to offer a pancake bar with a variety of toppings, as well as snacks and drinks of all sorts. And in return, guests bring an abundance of whatever it is they will give up for Lent, if that is their custom, or whatever is convenient. Hence, the fridge filled with six-packs.

Despite the fact that many of my friends have braved midweek, interborough subway rides to get to my apartment in Queens (the second most populous but by most twentysomethings' standards, at most the third most popular borough in New York), a couple dozen people have showed up. The motivational power of free pancakes should not be understated. And despite the holiday's reputation and the evidence in my fridge, no one is beyond buzzed; rather, everyone seems to move easily from the kitchen to the living room and from plate to plate, laughing and chatting and, occasionally, even talking about everyone's favorite topic of conversation at parties: Lent.

"What are you giving up?" a friend asks.

The Lenten fast is a topic I've thought about a lot, that I've actually planned for this year, that will likely be more challenging to complete—and to explain—than my Lenten practices of any year previous to this one. I will start by explaining the easy part.

"Alcohol," I say, "and sweets." I pause, trying to determine if I should go on. "And I'm going to try to complete all the Corporal Works of Mercy." Before I can explain what that means or mention that I also plan to attend the stations of the cross—twice—my friend interrupts.

"Wait, are you giving up all alcohol?" she asks. "Or just beer?"

"All of it," I say, cringing slightly in anticipation of her reaction.

"Don't do that," my friend says, only half joking.

And, for a second, I think that maybe she's right. Maybe it will make me look like a religious fanatic or preachy teetotaler. And if my friends who know me think it's crazy, I wonder what strangers will say. More specifically: What about potential dates, which, in New York, frequently take place at bars? How do I handle having to broach the topic of religious belief straight off the bat? For me, this is more of a social challenge than the not-drinking part. After all, my two favorite drinks are unlikely to impress: Baileys Irish Cream, which tastes like candy, and whiskey and ginger ale, which makes me seem like an elderly grandmother. (Although I could be wrong: my great aunt, upon hearing that I'd ordered a whiskey ginger ale at my cousin's wedding, proclaimed, "Don't you know ginger ale is bad for you?!") I open the fridge and hand out another bottle, hoping that by the end of the night I'll be able to fit some actual food in there. "We'll see," I say, and head into the living room in search of cookies.

In the hours before midnight, friends grin as they offer reminders of the amount of time remaining before Ash Wednesday, knowing that I don't want to find myself mindlessly snacking into the early hours of a day when I'm meant to eat, at most, three small meals. But it is not until after 11:00 p.m. that I begin to feel slightly anxious. My resolve starts to melt away as the season of Lent that lies ahead seems to stretch into infinity. I begin to rationalize away some of the upcoming sacrifices I'd felt good about earlier in the week. *Perhaps I will just give up beer. Perhaps just sweets.* I imagine all the scenarios in which I might break my fasts, and I recall past Lents when I have done so. (Jesus himself would have had a tough time turning down the two rooms—*rooms*—of desserts at my friend's wedding last year. Get behind me, Chocolate Fountain!) At the core of my worry is this: I won't be able to adhere to these sacrifices perfectly, so maybe I shouldn't try to adhere to them at all.

In an effort to avoid the temptations, I begin pushing bottles of wine and boxes of doughnuts and cookies into my guests' hands as they slowly head home for the night, emptying my apartment. It is close to midnight, and my friends Lauren and Zubair, and Lauren's boyfriend, Brett, are the last ones to go. I sip some of the homemade beer Brett brought with him and pick at some peanut M&Ms and hummus as we discuss movies and tell stories. I'm particularly excited that Lauren and Zubair came to the party. They joined the Rite of Christian Initiation of Adults program, commonly known as RCIA, at St. Paul the Apostle Church in Manhattan the previous fall and will make their confirmations this year. The next few weeks are especially important, as they represent a kind of homestretch. I am Lauren's sponsor, which means that I'm supposed to help guide her through the process, support her, and help answer any questions she might have. I worry sometimes that I don't know enough, that I won't have all the answers. In fact, I have plenty of questions myself: If I hadn't been raised Catholic, would I choose the faith today? Is the church really as welcoming a place as it could be? Am I doing all I can to live up to what is asked of me? They're questions that occur to me often, but I am hoping that the next forty days will be a time to think about them more deeply.

Our conversation shifts to RCIA, and Lauren expresses her admiration for Fr. Robert Collins, the Jesuit priest who directs the program. Zubair and I nod in agreement. If I had grown up in another faith and I'd wandered into a Catholic church hoping to learn more about it, Fr. Collins is the man I'd want to greet me. He somehow maintains the ability to be heartbreakingly sincere one moment and sidesplittingly sarcastic the next. He is consistent, diligent, smart, and humble. He is also my coworker at the magazine where I'm an editor—which is how, while standing around the editorial office one day, I was convinced to become a sponsor. I'd been uncertain, at first. But after spending the past several months talking to smart young people who chose to join the church, even after the scandals, even with its often unpopular views, I've grown enthusiastic about my role, and more encouraged in my own faith.

Just minutes before midnight, I wave good-bye to Lauren, Brett, and Zubair, calling after them, "Happy Almost Ash Wednesday!" as they make their way down the stairs. Soon, my clock blinks to midnight, and Lent officially begins. I look out over the empty bottles filling my kitchen and the plates filled with bits of food I am no longer allowed to eat. There is so much to get in order. There is so much to be done. I take a deep breath and decide to tackle it bit by bit. It is time to clean up the mess.

CHAPTER 2

—IN WHICH I WONDER WHETHER I SHOULD HAVE GIVEN A HOMELESS MAN MY TUNA SANDWICH

Despite my incessant e-mails and multiple phone calls (not to mention our country's sky-high incarceration rate), I was having a great deal of trouble getting into prison. I had applied to visit San Quentin State Prison in California as a reporter. The process involved several layers of approval, including a Catholic prison chaplain and a communications officer. I hoped to write a story on some theology classes being held for the inmates there and, while I was at it, to see the prison Johnny Cash immortalized in his song "San Quentin."

To be honest, my image of prison was the voices of the rowdy inmates that can be heard in the live version of the Cash song combined with the set of the Mayberry jail from *The Andy Griffith Show*. While I waited for a reply from the prison folks, I decided it was time for some actual research on correctional facilities and Catholicism. An Internet search and just a few clicks later, I came across a short but familiar list that connected the two topics: the Corporal Works of Mercy. I'd memorized this list in elementary school religion class, though several of them had seemed distant at the time. Now, almost age thirty, I realized that, although I could no longer rattle them off, they resonated with me:

- Feed the hungry
- Give drink to the thirsty
- Clothe the naked
- Harbor the harborless (aka shelter the homeless)
- Visit the sick
- Ransom the captive (aka visit the imprisoned)
- Bury the dead

At one time or another I'd done each of these, to some extent, but how often and how deliberately? I hoped to have the chance to complete one of them at San Quentin.

The Works of Mercy originate from Matthew 25:34–37, 40, in which Jesus spoke of the final judgment, saying:

> Then the king will say to those at his right hand, "Come, you that are blessed by my Father, inherit the kingdom prepared for you from the foundation of the world; for I was hungry and you gave me food, I was thirsty and you gave me something to drink, I was a stranger and you welcomed me, I was naked and you gave me clothing, I was sick and you took care of me, I was in prison and you visited me."

And then Jesus delivers the real kicker: "Truly I tell you, just as you did not do it to one of the least of these who are members of my family, you did not do it to me."

I looked back at the list. Occasionally I bought coffee for coworkers. Did that count as giving drink to the thirsty? Even if coffee tends to dehydrate? I decided I needed to start paying better attention to this list, not because I was afraid of the end times, but because I was afraid I'd stopped seeing Christ in the people mentioned. City life can do that to you sometimes. When you pass by thousands of people each week, it takes work to see Christ in all of them. I wondered if I'd been putting in the work.

For example, on any given day in New York, I might see any number of people who are homeless. I struggle constantly with how to respond to requests for money or food from people on the subway or the street. I have offered fresh food to people who say they are hungry, only to have them demand money. I have walked by women using cardboard boxes as blankets on the sidewalk and done nothing. I have refused to look people in the eye.

One cold winter night I bought a tuna sandwich for dinner at CVS pharmacy. I was hungry and late for a meeting and was feeling sorry for myself for having to eat dinner at a place that also sells panty hose and cold medicine. I passed a man curled up under some blankets on the street. "Got anything to eat?" he asked, clearly seeing that I did. I took out half of the sandwich and gave it to him. But as I walked away, doubts filled my head: *Should I have given him the whole sandwich? Should I have bought another one just for him? Was he even hungry?*

It's not easy to determine the best ways to act with kindness and mercy. Of course St. Basil the Great, of the fourth century, saw less grey area. He put it quite simply: "The bread which you do not use is the bread of the hungry; the garment hanging in your wardrobe is the garment of him who is naked; the shoes that you do not wear are the shoes of the one who is barefoot; the money that you keep locked away is the money of the poor; the acts of charity that you do not perform are so many injustices that you commit."

That's a challenging statement. My lack of action can be, in itself, an injustice. But how do we know when and how to act? While I felt guilty about the tuna sandwich incident, I also had been particularly wary of homeless men in recent months. The previous summer I had been threatened by a man who'd locked himself in the wheelchair-accessible bathroom at church. I knocked on the door to check on him and also because a friend in a wheelchair needed it. The man whipped open the door, a flurry of baggy, ragged clothes and unkempt hair.

Angry and screaming and delusional, he believed his feet had been burned by acid and that I'd been continually bothering him. His arm was raised and his fist clenched tightly as he started at me. All I can remember about that moment is thinking, *I'm about to get punched in the face*, although I made no attempt to move. Sensing this, my then-boyfriend stepped in to mediate, and the man punched him in the face instead. It was a long day.

But that was a while ago, and the man in the bathroom didn't represent all people struggling to live on the street. Perhaps, I thought, I could stand to show a bit more mercy toward them, as the list on my screen was urging me to do. Mercy, as described by Catherine McAuley, founder of the Sisters of Mercy, is "the principal path pointed out by Jesus Christ to those who are desirous of following Him." It sounds simple enough. And yet I often feel that this path can be a difficult one to travel, and that keeping pace with Jesus, our guide, is a challenge, especially when his directions so often come hidden within strange stories. But I also feel that it is a path worth pursuing, even if we end up wandering for a bit. The path of mercy is a wide one, with room to walk beside others. And as I reread that list of works, I realized the path of mercy was one I needed to walk more deliberately. And as long as I was committed to doing one work of mercy by visiting the prison, why not try to do them all? With Lent approaching, it seemed like the perfect time to start fresh. I started making a Works of Mercy to-do list.

Of course my plan had potential drawbacks, many of which flashed through my mind: It seemed foolish to try to do all of these acts in just a few weeks. Could I possibly do all of them well? Would my friends and family think I was overly pious—or worse, insincere? Doing the Works of Mercy poorly or as a stunt seemed worse than not doing them at all. Maybe there was no rush. I recalled a parable I'd read a few months back.

In late autumn the RCIA candidates and catechumens—the people who want to be baptized or confirmed in the Catholic Church as adults—start to learn about Scripture. As a sponsor, it is my job to help support them through the process. In the early sessions, one of our handouts was a paper with about fifteen parables listed on it: The lost sheep, the mustard seed, and the pearl of great price were among them. We were asked to choose between our favorite and our "un-favorite," because technically I don't think you're allowed to officially dislike the Word of God. The parable of the lost sheep ranked high on our group's favorites list, but the parable about the rich man and Lazarus ranked much lower.

The gist of that parable is this: Throughout his life, the rich man ignores Lazarus, and then (spoiler alert) the rich man dies and goes to hell. He asks if he can go back and warn his brothers and let them know that they may meet the same fate if they continue on the path they're on (they, too, are prone to ignoring the poor and sick), but the rich man is told no; the brothers may have the same tendencies, but they also get the same warnings the rich man received (Luke 16:19–31).

This story is not in line with the way most of us like to envision God or the afterlife. When we read this parable, we think that surely God must show some mercy here, and yet this God seems harsh. It's easy to think that God's mercy is a kind of get-out-of-jail-free card, but to consider it as such robs the term of its richness. We don't like to think about the times we ignore the poor. I'm not proud of the many times I've walked by people who are homeless without handing them even half of a tuna sandwich. But at the weekly RCIA meeting, another one of the sponsors surprised me by picking the Lazarus parable as a favorite. "It's a good reminder that there's only so much time," he said. And he's right. I likely have more than forty days left to complete the Corporal Works of Mercy. I hope to have many decades ahead of me, but I might not. And there's a difference between making sure I don't rush to complete the Works of Mercy and never actually getting started. Maybe God's mercy is evident in the fact that God gives us the time and free will to figure these things out for ourselves.

The thing is, it's easy to imagine yourself doing great works of mercy. It's easy to have good intentions. What's difficult is that follow-through, because God didn't challenge us to commit to the Corporal Works of Mercy for forty days. God challenges us to commit to a lifestyle—and a lifetime—of mercy. And that's not easy, because maybe in the end, the Works of Mercy aren't things that can be completed the way one can finish playing a board game or painting a picture. Each act is not an isolated incident, but a part of a process, akin to sweeping the floor. You have to do it regularly or things begin to get messy. They must become habits without becoming mindless. Ultimately, the Works of Mercy point us toward ways in which we can build God's reign on earth. There's no guarantee we get to see how it ends, but I know I certainly won't make progress if I don't begin.

I understand that trying to complete the Works of Mercy in a certain amount of time is potentially inconvenient or largely impractical. But so is much of the Christian life. It is easy for me to say that I will do these things . . . eventually, when the time is right. E. B. White once wrote, "A writer who waits for ideal conditions under which to work will die without putting a word on paper," and I think it's all too easy to fall into the same trap when it comes to our good deeds. We think: *I will start volunteering as soon as I finish getting the house clean, or finish a class as soon as my life is in order.* But life isn't always orderly. James Keenan, SJ, describes mercy as "the willingness to enter into the chaos of another," which doesn't necessarily mean you're not bringing a bit of your own chaos with you as well. So I began making a list of my own, the ways in which I could live out these works of mercy in a meaningful way.

At the Pancake Day Spectacular, someone had asked me, "Have you ever actually experienced spiritual growth by giving something up?" I had to pause. The answer was yes, but I wasn't sure why. If one could achieve spiritual enlightenment by abstaining from ice cream for forty days, life would be a lot easier.

"I guess it makes me redirect my thoughts to what's actually important," I said. At its best, giving something up is a good reminder to do something more. I thought of the many long days of Lent ahead of me, of the goals I had in place, and I hoped that this "more" would not become too much.

CHAPTER 3

—IN WHICH I AM HUNGRY, CRABBY, AND GRATEFUL ON ASH WEDNESDAY

As I'm waking up on Ash Wednesday morning, my first thought is how glad I am that I didn't decide to make morning workouts part of my Lenten routine. My normal coping mechanism after a late night—a vanilla iced latte—doesn't seem to be in the spirit of the traditional Ash Wednesday fast, so I walk past the coffee shop near my office and instead fill up my water bottle before sitting down at my desk.

The morning passes relatively quickly, and at noon I join my coworkers, Jesuit and lay, in the simple chapel on the fifth floor of our office building, which doubles as a Jesuit residence. One of the nice things about having priests for coworkers is that on days like this, I don't have to worry about missing Mass.

I read the first Scripture passage of the Mass (Joel 2:12–18), which is a cry for action, for vigilance, for repentance, which all sound somewhat frightening. But it is also a call for a return to a just God, to a God who—"perhaps"—will have mercy on us.

In the Gospel reading, I hear:

Beware of practicing your piety before others in order to be seen by them. . . . But when you fast, put oil on your head and wash your face, so that your fasting may be seen not by others but by your Father who is in secret.

—Matthew 6:1,17–18

I sit up a little straighter. It's strange to hear this and then to think about heading home through the city where everyone on the subway will see the ashes, which proclaim to the world: I am Catholic! I am fasting! Or, at the very least: I like going to church on days when they hand out free stuff. It sometimes seems oddly contrary to what this Gospel calls us to do. Still, public expression of religion isn't unusual in New York, and this is one of my favorite things about the city.

On any given day I might see the *payot* of Orthodox Jewish men trail out from under large black hats. A group of robed Hare Krishna singing and playing a tiny piano and finger cymbals while sitting on blankets in Union Square. On the subway, people with booming voices and ragged jackets proclaim the end of the world. The man running the halal cart lays out a piece of cardboard on the sidewalk as a prayer mat and faces Mecca. And with my ashes, I feel united with all of them in our shared path of faith.

Occasionally, I see an older Filipino woman clutching a rosary as she walks, or a teenage Latina girl reading her Bible. On the whole, though, Catholics aren't identifiable at first glance. Yet, on Ash Wednesday I'm always surprised by the number of people I see on the streets and in the subways sporting black smudges on their foreheads. And sometimes, despite the tacit but rarely broken code of not making eye contact on the subway, someone will notice your ashes and you'll exchange The Nod, a kind of half smile and tilt of the head that acknowledges that we're not as distant from each other as we think.

Of course there have been times when the black smudge felt more like it marked me as an outsider than inviting interaction or connection with others. During my junior year of college, I studied in England. On Ash Wednesday, I walked down the street a short while after having received my ashes, though already they had become slightly smudged and turned down at the corners of the cross. I happened to run into a British friend of mine. He looked at my forehead and then looked closer, appearing to show some concern. "Why," he asked politely, "do you have the Batman symbol on your forehead?"

And I am thinking of all these past Ash Wednesdays when the presider says, "Remember that you are dust and to dust you shall return—and hope in the resurrection." I feel the grain of the ashes settle onto my forehead. I am marked with the sign of the cross, and there, in our small community, I do indeed feel hope.

But by 3:37 p.m., my hunger has overwhelmed my hope. Almost all enthusiasm that I felt leading up to Lent is sapped. Despite my small bowl of soup for lunch, I am tired and crabby, and I am certain that I will feel exactly like this for the next forty days. Somehow I make it through the afternoon and walk through the cold to attend the weekly RCIA session, where Fr. Collins takes a few minutes toward the end of class to further discuss the liturgical season that is just beginning, and with which I am beginning to have a fraught relationship. He explains the concept of fasting to Jackie, Lauren, and Zubair: three small meals, two of which, when combined, do not equal the third. And, as always, he delves beyond the logistics into the larger context.

"Always make sure that last meal on Mardi Gras is pretty good," Fr. Collins says with a laugh. "But when you're fasting, you should feel a little uncomfortable. It allows you to cultivate a hunger for other things."

I know friends who derive great spiritual nourishment from fasting. Mostly I derive hunger pangs. I need to work on this, I think.

"For centuries we were told simply to avoid evil," Fr. Collins says. "But we must do good and avoid evil. People think: if I get to the end of the list of things not to do, and I haven't done them, I'm a good person. That just falls a little short of what we're called to do. It can't be everything; it has to spur you to do more."

CHAPTER 4

—IN WHICH I CONSIDER THE MEANING OF SACRIFICE

I am sitting on the couch eating sugar-covered cereal directly from the box and watching minor celebrities argue on reality TV. Technically, I am not breaking my Lenten sacrifice of not eating sweets. Sugary cereal isn't typically categorized with desserts such as pie, cake, candy, or ice cream. And yet I can't shake the feeling that such activities probably are a better way to get type 2 diabetes than they are a way to grow in my relationship with God.

The first time I swore off sweets completely during Lent was in eighth grade. I actually had less trouble sticking to it back then. With no job and no vehicle, I did not have the option of going to the grocery store. I just ate what my mother bought, and my Lenten snacks consisted almost entirely of Saltines and grapefruits.

But as an adult, I often just replace the sweets with another food, which, I'll confess, isn't really the point. Instead of detaching from the need to snack or allowing myself to be hungry in solidarity with the poor, I find myself arguing that Cinnamon Toast Crunch is not a dessert, but simply a breakfast cereal that I happen to be snacking on after dinner. No matter that it is literally covered in sugar. It does not take me long to find a Lenten loophole.

Despite all of this trouble, this overthinking, the potential for scrupulosity, I must confess: I love Lent. I love the sense of possibility the season implies. I love the symbolism that comes along with it. I love that it compels me to act, to change, to rethink how I am living, in a way that is more purposeful than at any other time of year. Of course, I must admit that this compulsion is, in part, due to the fact that I am highly motivated by guilt. And if I've promised God that I'm going to do something for forty days, I tend to try a bit harder to stick to it than if I've just made a promise to myself.

As a season of prayer, fasting, and almsgiving, Lent isn't at the top of everyone's list of favorite seasons. That's understandable. It's hard. You have to discern. You have to refrain from doing things you would normally do, and likely enjoy. And, often, you have to tell others why you are not doing them, thus risking discussing your religious beliefs with strangers. There is an abundance of spiritual tools and resources available for navigating these forty(ish) days, but there is otherwise little fanfare in the public square. I've never heard anyone complain about the crass commercialization of Lent or that the department-store Lenten displays seem to start earlier each year. And that's one of the reasons I like it.

Sure, if I make it through the forty days, I might find a basket filled with marshmallow Peeps and Cadbury eggs on Easter morning, but that's hardly enough motivation to change my ways. Children never hear threats of the Easter Bunny leaving coal instead of eggs if they don't keep their Lenten fast. So, I have to find my own reasons.

The season, in many ways, is a personal spiritual journey. The process of examining one's life and one's relationship with God offers rewards equal to what one puts into it. Yet Lenten sacrifices are more than simple attempts at self-improvement. This period of examination allows me to become a better member of my community. It gives me the space to ask: How do I use the absence of these comforts in order to feel the presence of God? How do I work toward a better under-standing of how to live out God's will for me? But, because I reside in one of the biggest (and arguably greatest) cities in the world, there's plenty to distract me from figuring this out.

Sometimes I wonder if my enthusiasm for Lent is misplaced. Given the words that kick off the season—"Remember that you are dust and to dust you shall return"—perhaps the giddy anticipation I feel while waiting in line for my ashes should be replaced by more somber reflec-tion. Lent not only gives me permission to rethink my life, but it also demands that I do so. And so I try. And every year, I imagine that this will be the one magical Lent that will fix all my faults—that, in the way Ben Franklin suggested tongue-in-cheek in his autobiography, I will work on my vices one by one, checking them off as I conquer them, rapidly approaching "moral perfection," as he put it, in just forty days. But then I realize that I actually have to follow through. Lent is a lot of things, but it isn't magic. And despite my general enthusiasm, it often can feel downright routine. I can recall only one Lenten season in the past seven years during which I have not given up some form of sweets. That other year I made the truly original decision to give up meat.

I wonder: what does it say about me that I'm giving up the same thing at age twenty-nine that I did when I was twelve? Much as I'd like to think that I was so spiritually advanced at twelve that I perfected the art of the meaningful Lenten sacrifice, I am pretty sure the answer is somewhat less flattering. And that's not to say I haven't tried to make Lent more meaningful, but somehow my sacrifice always sounds like a second attempt at a New Year's resolution. For example, one year I tried to give up sweets and cheese. I also tried to exercise more, read more, write more, and pray more. The "more," of course, is purpose-fully vague. If I wasn't exercising at all, technically once or twice during the month is an improvement.

I try not to be too hard on myself. I have often felt like my friend Kate, who once said to me: "Sweets are the only thing that work. I've tried other things. It's the only thing that's meaningful. Sweets are really difficult for me. It's Girl Scout cookie time; there are sweets all around my office; I have a chocolate stash. I remember that it's Lent. And every time I have to turn down sweets I think about Jesus."

Kate's comments bring up an intriguing question: how do I make Lent work for me? It's something I've wondered for a long time. But perhaps I haven't yet found an answer, because it's a question that's best answered by another question, one that goes beyond the forty days of the season: how do I let God work through me?

CHAPTER 5

—IN WHICH I AM COMPARED TO A TELEKINETIC, KILLER PROM QUEEN

When I first meet Jesús, he is standing on the sidewalk by the coffee cart wearing a grey hoodie and jeans. He is among a small group of people gathered to volunteer on the morning breadline at St. Francis of Assisi church on 34th Street in Manhattan. The breadline has been running continuously since the 1930s. Thousands of people have lined up for thousands of mornings to give and receive food here each day. Today is my first.

It is 6:45 a.m. on Monday morning of the first full week of Lent. I am standing in the cold, and I've been up for over an hour. Earlier, when I woke up in my overheated, third-floor walk-up in Queens, the darkness outside felt too dark and the lights in my apartment too bright. I had a stomachache, so I just rolled out of bed, ate Pepto-Bismol for breakfast, and headed to the subway. When I reached the elevated platform of the 7 train, the view of the Manhattan skyline was gorgeous and made the early wake-up seem worthwhile. The train was crowded, which surprised me. If I'd ever taken a moment to think about it, I'd have realized that out of the millions of New Yorkers, there are at least a few who ride the subway at 6:00 a.m. Yet that fact is easy to forget, considering it sometimes feels like every person in Queens is on the train with me at 8:30 a.m. during my usual commute.

Now, still slightly groggy, I am doing my best to make a good first impression. A line of people, mostly men, wraps along the side of the church wall. Behind an iron gate stands a man in a red ski jacket and another man in a red and black Kansas City Chiefs cap and brown leather jacket that reads "Radio City" over the left breast. "Excuse me," I say. "I'm here to volunteer for the breadline."

"Talk to this man right here," says the man in the red parka, whose name turns out to be Henry. "This is Don." The man in the Radio City jacket turns and welcomes me. "We start at seven," he says, before urging me to get some coffee. "We already have milk and sugar in it," he warns. "It's easier that way." I grab a Styrofoam cup from a small room a few steps down behind the gate. A table in the center holds plastic tubs filled with sandwiches and juice boxes, packed in plastic grocery bags. "The cardinal was here last week," Henry tells me when I return. "There were media all on the other side of the street," Don adds. I'm aware of this, actually, because I'd learned about the breadline from a photo of Cardinal Timothy Dolan in an Irish cap on the front page of *Catholic New York*, the archdiocesan newspaper.

"Jim will be here soon," Don says. "You can start out standing behind him and watching, and then you can start handing out bags during the second round." I'm slightly insulted that he thinks I don't know what to do, but the feeling later gives way to relief when I realize, in fact, I have no idea what to do. We are all huddled around a black cart with two shelves, onto which are stacked black plastic tubs filled with white plastic bags that have sub sandwiches and apple-juice drink boxes in them. There are about 450 sandwiches, Don tells me. And everyone gets *one*. At least at first.

"If they want another one, they have to go around to the end of the line," he says firmly. "I don't care what they say—man, woman, or child. I believe in equal opportunity for everyone." I nod.

Moments later, Jim arrives and introduces himself, then points his thumb at Don, laughs, and says, "I work for him."

"And I work for the brothers," Don says, referring to the Franciscans. He pauses. "And they work for God; it's trickle down. But by the time the blessings get to me, there's hardly any left." He grins as if to say he doesn't mind.

I introduce myself to Jim.

"Just think of blood," Don says to Jim with a smile.

"Blood?" Jim says. I look equally confused. I worry that already I have given the impression of being some sort of murderer. I think that maybe I should have showered before leaving the house.

"Yeah, like Carrie." He says. "You know, the prom?"

Ah, *Carrie*. The movie with the girl and the prom and the pig blood. I'm OK with this mnemonic device if it means he'll remember my name. No need to point out that the spelling is different.

Just then a bell tolls. "Here we go," Don says, and he walks forward, pulling the cart behind him. Henry is to the left in front of me, and Jim is to his right. Behind us is Jesús, who keeps the cart steady. The people stand in two parallel lines, and we push through the center. As we walk, the men hand out sandwiches as fast as they can. Nearly everyone we pass looks bedraggled, but a few people are dressed in crisp business casual and might be on their way to an office. Some pull suitcases or carry duffle bags. Almost all have heavy coats or hats and are unshaven. I say good morning, but most of the men won't make eye contact. A few keep their hands out after they pass Henry, hoping I'll give them a second bag. "Go around," Don keeps repeating, trying to maintain fairness. "We didn't get any!" say two old men, holding plastic bags and raising their arms in protest. I pause and then give them each a sandwich from the back of the cart. I don't know if that was the right thing to do or not.

Partway down the block, we stop. The sea of people has turned into a single line returning for seconds. Jim calls to me. "Stand here," he says, pointing to a spot in front of him, and I begin handing out sandwiches to the people waiting for seconds. I grab two at a time. A few people come by for thirds. And then, by 7:15, the whole thing is over. The men patiently wait in two lines to fill up Styrofoam cups at the two large silver tanks of coffee on the sidewalk, and it reminds me of the sort of coffee hours parishes often hold after Mass.

The sandwich cart is wheeled back to the storage room. Henry points out some lockers to me and says that I can leave my purse there in the future and that there's a bathroom around the corner. They all seem to expect that I'll come back. And, despite the early morning wake-up call, I want to.

"Stay away from pig's blood!" Don calls out to me as I walk up the steps into the chapel.

"I tend to try to," I say, laughing.

Inside the church, Henry has taken his position as an usher and holds the collection basket at the ready. I walk over to a side altar filled with mosaics of St. Anthony and a large statue of what I assume is meant to look like his dead body in a tomb. I kneel down but am not particularly inspired by the fake plaster body in front of me. I prefer the colorful tile mosaic on the side wall of Anthony preaching to the fish: no less strange, but slightly less gruesome. St. Anthony is perhaps best known today for being patron saint of lost things, but he was also known in his time as a great preacher, who easily captured the attention of his listeners. Legend says that even the fish popped their heads out of the water to hear him. I look down in front of the kneeler and notice a wicker basket containing a few dollars and several scraps of paper with tiny notes on them. I can see "Dear St. Anthony" scrawled on some of them. Others are folded many times, small enough to look like trash but with enough visible to see that they have notes—prayers—too.

After only two early mornings, I am already starting to feel tired, and I'm still not sure where this Lenten journey is taking me or how much I'll be helping anyone. So I just concentrate on the moment. I pray for the people who have left their petitions here, for the volunteers, for the men drinking warm coffee outside, for the man who took three sandwiches, for those who have none, and, looking up at the image of St. Anthony, for all who are lost.

CHAPTER 6

—IN WHICH I PULL A SANDWICH CART WITH JESÚS

On Tuesday, the morning feels even darker than the day before and the subway slightly less novel. The idea of being a morning person greatly appeals to me; in practice, I have great difficulty. Today Henry sports a black satin firefighter jacket with his name stitched into the front and a shamrock on the other side over the firefighter seal. Don is wearing, as far as I can tell, the same thing as the day before. This time, everyone is already in the room downstairs that is filled with crates of juice boxes when I arrive.

"Well, I'll be," Don says when I show up, marking the first time I've ever heard someone use that phrase without irony. A bearded man in a knit cap has shown up today as well, and there are too many volunteers. It seems like a nice problem to have. "Jesús, you want to pull the cart today?" Don asks. Jesús agrees. Don leaves without much fanfare, and I'm placed toward the front of the cart today on the left. Jim is at the right, and Henry moves behind me. The man in the cap mans the back and refills the buckets. Jesús pulls the coffee cart.

I feel like I'm part of some strange, slow-moving train about to chug along 34th Street. We move forward, immersing ourselves in this sea of humanity on all sides. As on the previous day, some of the men in the line begin to circle back. I notice one guy—tall, with curly hair and a camel-hair trench coat—coming back several times. He is supposed to get in the other line, the one for seconds.

I don't like the idea of denying someone food on a breadline, but I don't like the idea of someone breaking the rules either. I find myself feeling annoyed. I don't want to say anything and make a scene on the second day, so I just give him a dirty look and a sandwich. But I wonder if a Work of Mercy still counts if you're crabby about it.

I want to trust this man. I am the type of person who wants to trust everyone. I want to be one of the "righteous" in Matthew's Gospel, without being self-righteous. I want to ask, "When did I see you hungry and feed you?" And I want to know in my heart that the answer is in these men, hands outstretched.

I try to remember to say "Good morning" to each person. One man in a hood looks up and tells me to have a blessed day. He seems like maybe he could play a guardian angel with a Brooklyn accent in an inspirational film. I half expect him to vanish as he walks down the street. My annoyance melts away, and I realize that I was hoping for a bit more of that kindness. People who are homeless can easily be found throughout the city, and at some point every New Yorker has to choose how he or she will react. It seems like too much, sometimes, to feel for every person you see and to give to people not knowing what they'll do with the money. Some people walk by. Some people help. It is difficult to see everyone as an individual, and as of late, I have tended to view homeless men and women as belonging to one of two extremes: Christ figures or crazy people.

When the sandwiches are gone, I say good-bye and walk over to 5th Avenue and then up to St. Patrick's for 7:30 a.m. Mass. I'm a few minutes late, which is actually quite a good chunk of a morning Mass that lasts only twenty minutes. But I make it in time for the Gospel, which in Catholic lore means that it still "counts." I sit in a pew behind a guy who looks about my age and also appears attractive and like maybe he has a job. I do not go to Mass to find potential dates, but it's not a bad bonus, and I figure God helps those who strategically seat themselves.

I still find it kind of amazing that on any given day I can walk into a local church and find Timothy Dolan, archbishop of New York and one of the most influential Catholics in the United States, celebrating Mass. His homily, which lasts only a few minutes, talks about the need for both prayer and charity and that each is hollow without the other. "In prayer, love of God. In charity, love of neighbor," he says. And I think back to the faces in the breadline and wonder if these two statements are actually saying the same thing. And I'm so engrossed in thinking about this that I don't even worry about whether or not the cute guy who may have a job is trying to catch my eye at the sign of peace.

Later that day, while at the office, I find myself trying to strike bargains with God: I fed the homeless twice this week, that's got to be worth at least one cookie at lunch. But the words from Mass, at least the part I made it to, stick in my head: *Grant us through these mysteries, Lord, that by moderating earthly desires we may learn to love the things of heaven through Christ our Lord.* In the end I resist breaking my fast so early in the process, but perhaps more out of exhaustion than piety.

The French philosopher and activist Simone Weil once wrote: "Over the infinity of space and time, the infinitely more infinite love of God comes to possess us. He comes at his own time. We have the power to consent to receive him or to refuse. If we remain deaf, he comes back again and again like a beggar, but also, like a beggar, one day he stops coming." Here she does not mean that God abandons us, but that God plants a seed of faith in us, which we must allow to grow and accept and say yes to. But in order to let God in, we have to have the energy to get up and open that door. Tonight, instead, I fall asleep.

CHAPTER 7

—IN WHICH I WITNESS A MODERN-DAY TRANSFIGURATION

St. Patrick's Cathedral, with its glorious arches, complex stained glass, and the galeri hanging from the ceiling, always feels more stately than homey when compared with other churches in the city. To me, the edifice sometimes seems to be to the archdiocese of New York what the Empire State Building is to the city itself: a kind of iconic symbol of its grandeur, history, and beauty, but not a place frequented by the locals. And if St. Patrick's is like the Empire State Building, then my local parish is more like a bodega, the neighborhood spot where you run into people you know as you make your weekly stop for necessities. So in a way, it seemed strange to attend Mass at the cathedral with the RCIA crew on this second Sunday of Lent. Until that point, our small group had seemed parish-based. While we all knew that the candidates—people who already have been baptized into Christian faith—were working toward full communion with the Catholic Church, the local parish at St. Paul's was where everything actually happened.

But as we file through the giant doors of St. Patrick's and find our pew, labeled "row 28" (on the south side of the church in the side aisle with a good view of the cardinal's chair), the church seems more like what it was meant to be: the parish of the whole city. Any New Yorker can walk in the door at almost any time and immediately belong.

We pick up our bilingual programs, which read on the front: "Rite of Calling the Candidates to Continuing Conversion." It is a ceremony at which all the local candidates gather together with their sponsors and the local bishop to recognize the candidates' readiness to join the church. I have never seen St. Patrick's so full of people. Each pew is labeled, and each parish group huddles together looking both joyful and nervous. I think about the individual journeys that brought each person to this place—the decisions, the troubles, the graces that occurred to bring us all together, those things that enable us to make a leap of faith.

But maybe a "leap" isn't the most appropriate metaphor for this spiritual journey. As the program states, we are called to "continuing conversion." We do not simply just fall deeper and deeper into our faith after our baptism or initial conversion. We are called to keep jumping. We talk of that "leap of faith," but our reality is one of multiple leaps, every day. Tiny jumps, or steps, even, sometimes just the distance it takes for our feet to go from the bed to the floor. It is that forward motion that keeps us going, that keeps saying that today will be better. Today I will try harder. Today I might fail. But I am still loved. It is why I set my alarm to get up to go to the breadline even after sleeping in a few days in a row, because sometimes having faith simply means, to steal Samuel Beckett's words, to "fail better."

The rite begins, and from a well-lit altar, a Gospel passage is read:

> [L]ater, Jesus took with him Peter and James and his brother John and led them up a high mountain, by themselves. And he was transfigured before them, and his face shone like the sun, and his clothes became dazzling white. Suddenly there appeared to them Moses and Elijah, talking with him. Then Peter said to Jesus, "Lord, it is good for us to be here; if you wish, I will make three dwellings here, one for you,

one for Moses, and one for Elijah." While he was still speaking, suddenly a bright cloud overshadowed them, and from the cloud a voice said, "This is my Son, the Beloved; with him I am well pleased; listen to him!". . . . And when they looked up, they saw no one except Jesus himself alone.

—Matthew 17:1–5, 8

The Gospel is followed by a homily by Cardinal Dolan, who has only recently been named as such. He tells of how the experience of being named a cardinal, while tempting him to pride, has humbled him. On his trip to Rome, he visited the Sistine Chapel with a number of people from the archdiocese of New York, and found himself beaming in his new robes. But as he walked into the chapel, the first thing he sees, of course, is Michelangelo's fresco *The Last Judgment*. The image struck him and he had a kind of revelation.

"I am thinking to myself: When I stand before the judgment seat of Christ the King, *this* isn't going to do me a bit of good at all." He points to his scarlet zucchetto, a skullcap that signifies his status. "Because Christ is not going to care if I'm a cardinal. He's not even going to call me 'your eminence.' He's going to say: 'Have you fed the poor? Have you clothed the naked? Have you helped the sick? Have you looked after the children? Have you taught the ignorant? Have you visited those in prisons? Have you treated those in need as if they were me?' Talk about bringing me back down to earth!"

I don't know when my own judgment day will come. And as I reflect on my actions of late, I honestly don't know if, after Lent, or after a lifetime, I'll be able to truly answer yes to those questions in a way that denotes the kind of constant, deliberate attention to the poor that Christ is asking for. But at the very least, I'll be able to say that I tried.

After the homily it is time for the "Call to Continuing Conversion." One by one, the RCIA directors or priests from each parish walk up to a microphone in the center aisle and proclaim a personalized form of the statement: "St. Paul the Apostle Church happily presents the candidates from our parish!" And the thing is, they really do seem happy. Large groups stream into the aisle and take their place in the sanctuary behind the altar. Fr. Collins calls our group about halfway through, and we go up and take our place. The lights on the altar are surprisingly bright, and the crowd seems to glow. The names continue to be read out, and the groups stream on either side of the altar. Some hold up children to the cardinal for a blessing as he passes them by. He places his hat on their heads. Soon there are more people on the altar than in the pews, and I wish that everyone could have this perspective at some time. Too often there is such a sense of separation between parishioners and the altar; it feels more like a place from which we receive rather than one at which we gather or to which we, too, can contribute. All of us up there together, loving, questioning, shining, and transforming, turn the crowd into a community. And suddenly, looking around, in every face I see no one except Jesus.

CHAPTER 8

—IN WHICH I AM ADVISED WHERE "NOT TO MEET MEN"

It is Thursday during the second full week of Lent, and for the first time, I do not even consider getting up for the breadline or Mass. I'm just too tired. *How does one make the Works of Mercy count without burning out?* I think, as I burrow deeper beneath my comforter.

That evening, I attend my Mercy Associates meeting, where we discuss ecology and creation. The Mercy Associates is a group of lay women and men who pledge to live out the charism of Mercy through a commitment to community, prayer, and justice. When I read about the group for the first time, it occurred to me that this is what the woman in the sweatshirt with the nature scene—the woman who had complimented my shoes during my volunteer interview so many years earlier—had been. I am in the process of discerning whether or not to become a full member. I'm far from the ideal Catholic, and at times joining the group seems like a big commitment. At other times, less so. As one friend put it: "So you're pledging to do stuff you should be doing anyway?" I suppose she's right, but it's easier to remember to do those things when you have some support. And already I have been encouraged by the community I've found in my fellow associates and in the sisters.

The Sisters of Mercy see the associates not only as helpers or friends but also as equals on the journey. Together we are living out the charism of mercy. "You give us hope," they say to me. And while I'd like to think it's because I've said something wise, it is more likely the simple fact that I am a twenty-nine-year-old woman and I go to Mass. Their statement seems funny because I have so much doubt some-times—in myself, in the church, in the way things are or will be. And yet even this doubt can bring comfort: I remind myself that Jesus fre-quently showed great faith in imperfect followers.

If all goes as planned, I'll join in a few months. My Lenten practice of exploring the Works of Mercy has become a part of my discernment process. I'm thinking more deliberately about the charism of the group I'm about to join. What does it mean to be merciful? Does it mean giving everything away? Does it mean risking being taken advantage of? Catherine McAuley once said, "It is better to relieve a hundred imposters than to suffer one truly deserving person to be sent away empty."

In joining the Mercy Associates I would be committing to prayer, community, and ministry in my life. The Sisters of Mercy also take a pledge to support me in these efforts. The practical, formal aspect of it is fairly simple and consists of monthly meetings and an occasional retreat. The hard part, of course, is internalizing these values and living them out. Despite my friends' suspicions (and, I suspect, the sisters' hopes), it does not mean I am on the way to becoming a nun. In fact, both men and women are welcome to become Mercy Associates, and my group in Glendale, Queens, is a varied bunch, ranging from work-ing parents to a 102-year-old woman who participates from a nursing home. I'm younger than many of my fellow associates, but the diver-sity of age and experience in our group offers interesting perspectives.

After the meeting, I call my mom as I walk from the subway to my apartment. Despite constant warnings about cell phone theft in New

York, I have made a habit of calling my parents while walking home. It has reached the point where my mom greets me with, "Hi, where are you headed?"

I describe the meeting to her, and she replies, "Were there any young people there?" The next youngest is in his forties probably, and I tell her as much.

"You should write an article called 'Where Not to Meet Men.'" She offers examples: the Mercy Associates meeting, an anti-death penalty meeting I'd attended, the breadline.

"Thanks, Mom," I say, ending one of the less helpful conversations we've had about my dating life. I know she's joking. Sort of. And on some level she's right. I used to think about my dating prospects more intentionally: *Where are good places to meet people?* But I realized that being the kind of person that people want to meet means being happy and being myself. So I go to the places I want to go. And it turns out that my interests align nicely with those of retirees. I've attended sewing classes and walking tours of historic homes alongside many a kindly old couple, who tell me I remind them of their grandchildren and that I should be grateful I still have my knees. But I'm happy. The way I see it is that either I'm eventually getting married or I'm not. And if it's eventually going to happen, I want to make sure not to squander this unique sort of freedom I have now, to take the time to enjoy activities that I might become too busy for or may not be able to commit to if I have a husband and children. And if I don't get married, then that's just as good a reason not to squander this time, because this is all the time I have. So, when my brother called me and offered a code for a free subscription to an online dating site, I clung to my laissez-faire approach to dating and immediately refused. I did not want this sort of charity from my younger brother. Then I paused. Then I agreed.

Online dating had been an interesting experience, thus far. I chose photos, wrote a profile, and assured my mother I would not let myself be murdered. I'd scrolled through countless profiles of men claiming to "work hard and play hard" and love family and the New York Yankees. I'd actually managed to go on a few dates. The whole experience had been less humiliating than I'd expected and, for the most part, sort of fun. But lately I haven't had much time to think about it; my plans for the Works of Mercy took priority over planning dates.

Knowing that these tasks are ahead of me gives me a strange sense of order and purpose. Even though I am busier than ever, my days feel more deliberate. I'm doing these works because I want to. In fact, the thing I dreaded most, giving up sweets, for fear that I'd need them to help get me through the long days, has in a way been the easiest part. Still, there are moments: the night when I was incredibly exhausted and attempting to finish a freelance assignment, when really all I wanted to do was eat cookies or ice cream and curl up on the couch. I wanted comfort, and I am beginning to recognize that those things don't cut it anymore.

It's easy to feel broken down in these first weeks of Lent, or any time, when trying to balance the things we want to do with the things we should do, and trying to create as much overlap between the two as possible. And above all, trying to unite these things with God's will for us. Catherine McAuley wrote a prayer that serves as a good reminder that part of this process is letting go:

> My God, I am yours for time and eternity. Teach me to cast myself entirely into the arms of your loving Providence with a lively, unlimited confidence in your compassionate, tender pity. Grant, O most merciful Redeemer, that whatever you ordain or permit may be acceptable to me. Take from my heart all painful anxiety; let nothing sadden me but sin, nothing delight me but the hope of coming to the possession of You my God and my all, in your everlasting kingdom. Amen.

At the end of the day, I get on my knees—the ones I'd been told by elderly couples to be grateful for—bless myself, and take that doubt and anxiety and give it up.

CHAPTER 9

—IN WHICH I CONTEMPLATE MY EARLY FASHION SENSE AND MY CURRENT CLUTTER

During my senior year of high school my mom and dad bought an ad in my honor in the yearbook, as many parents did, congratulating me on my graduation. It featured a photo of me at about age four, standing near the neighbor's garage that bordered our old backyard. I'm wearing shorts, rain boots, and a striped T-shirt and holding a clear umbrella opened over my shoulder. (It is not raining.) I'm also wearing a scarf and a knit winter cap with a pompom and earflaps and a string that tied below my chin. (It is summer.) I have apparently decided that the cap should be worn at a jaunty angle, or else I just don't care, because one of the earflaps is closer to covering my cheek than my ear. Despite all this I am clearly thrilled. Underneath the photo were the words: "Kerry, you've always had your own special style. Keep on grinning and going your own way. We love you so much."

My friends have often considered my sense of style a bit quirky. As a cross-country runner in high school, I was required to wear slightly ridiculous-looking purple shorts on a regular basis, so perhaps I just decided to embrace that spirit in my daily wardrobe. I wore retro blouses from Goodwill and resurrected T-shirts from childhood.

Because these T-shirts were huge on me when I first bought them, they fit appropriately and ironically as a teen.

Now, more than a decade later, I live in New York, arguably the fashion capital of the world, and I couldn't care less about that aspect of the city. It's not that I don't try to dress appropriately or, on occasion, fashionably; it's just that my interpretation of that has sometimes not quite been in sync with the mainstream tastes. To be fair, I didn't have to think about it too much growing up. At age five I shed the boots and lopsided hat for a plaid jumper and a button-down shirt and wore some approximation of that for the next thirteen years of parochial school. My high school was perhaps the only one in America at which girls got in trouble for wearing their skirts too long. I don't know how or when the style began, but the favored way to wear the grey wool skirts was as close to your ankles as possible. We were not allowed to wear printed T-shirts beneath our blouses, nor were we allowed to wear blouses that didn't bear the Cathedral High School logo. No flip-flops, sneakers, bandanas, or hats. We expressed our originality mostly through socks and, in my case, unusual home-made jewelry, such as necklaces made from buttons or hair bows that sang Christmas carols.

Wearing uniforms was kind of awesome, as it meant never having to worry about what you were wearing in the morning, and never having to do back-to-school shopping. I wore two skirts in four years. With such limited choices, I didn't worry much about wearing the wrong thing. Of course, I worried about a host of other things instead, just not clothes. I liked that the skirts were warm in the winter, although the same property held for summer, which I liked less.

Despite my love of the uniform, I still joined my classmates in longing for the one or two days a year when we were allowed a dress-down day. I still recall feeling especially cool my freshman year when I wore a long-sleeved T-shirt with a logo from a cross-country meet and a pair of blue-and-green-plaid pajama pants to class. My senior year, I was slightly more rebellious—or at least quirky. A friend and I decided that we would buy the dress-down day pass (money went to a charity) and then break every uniform rule possible. And there would be nothing anyone could do about it. (This is about as rebellious as I got. I will not be writing a scandalous tell-all about my adolescence anytime soon.) So on went the tie-dye T-shirt beneath the non-sanctioned white oxford blouse (for extra tie-dye visibility); on went the bandana and the flip-flops; and off we went to saunter around the school. I'm fairly certain most people didn't actually notice.

As original as New York is, certain neighborhoods or groups of people still seem to stick to an unofficial uniform. The hipsters in skinny jeans and sunglasses. The pencil skirts in Midtown. And it's a safe bet that on nearly any street in Manhattan, you'll see someone dressed in all black.

I struggle with how much attention I should devote to choosing what I wear each day. If given a choice, I'll most often be in jeans and a T-shirt. At the same time it's a common belief that what we wear is an outward sign of the respect we have for others and even how we want to represent ourselves to others. (So my message, I guess, would be this: I want to be comfortable.)

It's undeniable that when I do dress up, when I wear a gown or a business suit, I feel a bit different somehow.

Clothes can send a powerful symbol. St. Francis stripped off his own clothes to make a statement, to symbolically shed the life he planned to leave behind. Many women religious and clergy wear habits so that they might distinguish their life choice and be easily identified, so that people might seek them out for guidance or feel safe, as fellow passengers on an airplane. Other nuns and priests dress more like laypeople in an effort to make people comfortable and to seem less like the "other." Clothes matter, and yet we can't be too attached to them. We have to be willing to separate who we are from what we wear.

Christ said that if someone asks for your coat, give them your shirt as well. Some interpretations of this teaching argue that this is a way to embarrass the other person, that you'd end up naked before them, which, in Jesus' time, would have been more shameful for them than for you. But it also fits with Jesus' message that we have to be willing to give what we have, and sometimes to give to a point of discomfort.

I'm thinking about how much I really need in my own closet as I consider how I will "clothe the naked" during Lent. I begin to take an inventory. I already went through my closet in good faith a few weeks back in an effort to do some spring cleaning. So finding a lot more items to give away now might be a stretch. I need to come up with something more realistic. In my first purge of the closet, I got rid of the following:

- Three belts
- Five pairs of shoes (three dressy, two sneakers)
- Two sweaters
- One pair of corduroy pants
- One dress shirt
- Two old messenger bags
- Two lanyards from a convention
- A mouse pad
- A bracelet
- A tote bag

If I count the items I already got rid of, perhaps I can give away seven more items, or maybe twelve or some other biblically significant number. "Forty" comes to mind, given the forty days of Lent, but it seems like too much. It's not like I am always buying new clothes, I think.

Perhaps it is OK to hang on to my extra clothes, as long as they are older and inexpensive.

During high school we were told—warned really—that when we left the school grounds in our uniforms, when we wore them at Friendly's restaurant after school or while on a field trip, we were representing Cathedral High School, that how we behaved while wearing these uniforms represented the larger group of students. Which makes me wonder: what about the clothes I don't wear, but still hold on to; what do they say about me?

In Colossians, we're told to clothe ourselves with love, over everything else, over whatever styles we're wearing, over whatever ways we're seeking to define or distinguish ourselves. Like a less itchy and less tangible version of a Catholic school uniform, this love unites us. And the way we wear that love represents the larger group of Christians. It is up to each of us to make it unique in the way we live out that love—the spiritual version of wearing goofy socks and homemade jewelry—but this love must have at its core the same basic pieces. "They will know we are Christians by our Love," we are told. But only if we wear it well.

CHAPTER 10

—IN WHICH I REALIZE I DON'T NEED AS MANY CLOTHES AS I THOUGHT

"We have close to thirty women out there, so brace yourselves," Myrna says. She is a petite woman dressed in black, her dark hair pulled back by a headband with birds printed on it. A thin scarf hangs loosely around her neck. I lean on an old blue-and-white metal table that looks like it belongs in a 1950s kitchen; Lena stands beside me, a blonde volunteer who sports a grey Henley, jeans, and a German accent. She's in her early twenties. We are in the center of a small room in Maryhouse, the Catholic Worker community on the Lower East Side of Manhattan, during the second week of Lent. Both women live at St. Joseph House, the other Catholic Worker house a few blocks away, but are here today to work.

The vibrancy of the neighborhood seems far off, as there are no windows and the door to the room is shut. Women file through the heavy front door and enter an adjacent lunchroom. About forty women a day come Tuesday through Friday for free lunch and showers. One of the central tenets of the Catholic Worker Movement, founded by Dorothy Day in 1933, is hospitality (along with voluntary poverty and clarification of thought), and this open-door policy is an example of that principle in action. After lunch, the women have the option of entering the space in which we're standing, which is lined with old wooden shelves and metal racks filled with a wide variety of clothing. It is known, appropriately, as the Clothing Room.

Each woman is allowed to fill one plastic shopping bag with clothes and also to take a blanket and a coat. Lena, Myrna, and I are here to watch, to keep a kind of order. Otherwise, Myrna says, some of the people would take as much as they could. Myrna holds a plastic oatmeal tub in her hand filled with paper slips with numbers on them. Outside, the women in the lunchroom have numbers matching the ones in the tub, and soon Myrna will call them into the room a few at a time. "They have five minutes," Myrna explains. "We can't allow them to take advantage. We have to enforce fairness; just remind them of the time." I feel strange about being tasked with telling people I don't know that they can't take free clothes I don't own.

Large handwritten signs in purple ink label the sections by clothing sizes. The walls not covered with dark wooden shelves are covered in pale, pale blue paint. A metal shelf holds jeans and trousers. Coats are hung up by a side wall. Shoes lined up against the back. A table to the right holds an assortment of leftovers: hand-knit scarves, jigsaw puzzles, candle holders, old books, and a tiny green felt purse with an appliqué of Santa Claus on the front. Everything in the room has been donated.

We straighten the shelves and align the pairs of shoes to prepare for the big arrival. Despite its small size, there's a dignity and order to the room that conveys to the visitors that they are worth preparing for. The door opens and the first few women walk through. It's not exactly Black Friday, but there's an air of urgency, the sense that there are valuable items to unearth. Soon one woman's bag is overflowing. Lena calmly asks the woman to take out a few items so that everyone gets a fair amount. "You are not nice," the woman replies coldly.

After a few minutes, people begin to knock or try to open the door, but Myrna remains steadfast. After their quick survey of the room, many of the women begin to linger as the new group comes in. Most of the women are friendly and relaxed. One woman in a floral sweater and fashionable leggings rests her purse on the table. Another woman in a denim newsboy cap, her eyes streaked with blue eyeliner, looks up and issues a general warning: "Don't put your bags down." She says this not in a scolding manner but in a way that conveys weathered experience and genuine concern for—and wariness of—her neighbor. The woman in the floral sweater tucks her purse under her arm. "Thank you," she replies.

A tiny woman wearing a red shirt covered by a black felt vest comes up to where I'm standing at the side of the room, trying to stay out of the way. Her wrinkled face is framed by dark hair, one large section of it sticking out from the side of her head. She wordlessly points to the green Santa Claus purse. "This?" I ask, and she nods. The tiny bells jingle as I pull it from the nail and hand it to her.

A moment later, a woman's large frame, covered by a brown coat, blocks the doorway. "These are the only jeans that fit me," she says, clinging to the dark denim. I can see that her plastic bag is already full. "That's fine," Myrna says, "but you'll have to leave something else behind. We have to be fair." The women are able to come in for a second round after everyone has had a first look. Myrna says she can pick up the jeans on the second round. The woman's brown coat twirls as she spins on her heels and walks out.

Another woman's bag also has too many clothes, but the extras are kids' clothes she's trying to stuff into the bags. Some of the women are looking for office wear and sort through the dress slacks. I try to help a woman find a small pair of jeans. One woman in a maroon cap comes in and lingers. As we usher out her group, I tell her she can come back again at the end.

A woman with dark lip liner lays out a child's white sweater with a popcorn stitch. "Cute," I say. "It's for my granddaughter," she says.

"She's five. I always have to bring something for her when I see her."
I think of my own grandmother, my mom's mom, who felt the same
way about her grandchildren. I remember the time in first grade when,
after I spent several minutes petting the sleeve of a white, faux-rabbit-
fur coat in Blakes department store, my mother had to forcefully per-
suade her own mother not to buy it for me. And I wonder where each
of these items came from—if, perhaps, some of them were purchased
by grandmothers for grandchildren and then were given away as those
children grew, only to be passed on to the mothers and grandmothers
in front of me.

The woman holding number 13 wants only a pillow. "Did I call
your number?" Myrna asks. "Don't take that tone with me," Number
13 says in reply. "I just want a pillow," the woman repeats. I look on
the shelf, and the only one left is lumpy and reminds me of something you'd find under a bed at a youth hostel. Still, I want to hide
the pillow so that this woman is guaranteed to get it. She continues to wait outside while another woman enters wearing an oversized
Miami Heat jersey with the number 3 on the back. "I need a coat," she
says. "I'm just moved up from Florida." She has one long, thick braid
coming out of the top of her head and then pressed against the back
of her skull under a black cap. She throws on a giant, olive-colored,
double-breasted trench coat over a red-and-grey-plaid flannel shirt,
which she is wearing over her jersey, which is over a T-shirt. "Does this
fit?" she asks the crowd, in general. And for a second it feels like we're
all in a department store dressing room, offering advice as one occasionally does. No one is fighting each other for items, just assessing
and then complimenting. She decides to take the coat.

And then, suddenly it's time to close the Clothing Room.

"Sorry, ladies," Lena says. "Your time is up."

"You don't have to be sorry," says a woman in a black hat and coat.

That night, when I get home, I take a second look at my closet, and suddenly the items that seemed so necessary before seem extraneous. I hold up an old polyester shirt printed with blue and green flowers. I ask myself: *If someone from Maryhouse asked me for this, what would I say?* I can't remember the last time I wore it. If someone asked me why I still had it, I wouldn't have a ready answer. I push through a few more items. Some are from times when I was thinner, and to look at them reminds me of a size I hoped to be again someday. Others are from times when I was heavier and are now too large, but they remind me of special events or places I traveled to while wearing them.

I pick up a thin brown sweater with colorful golf tees embroidered across the front and the words "It's tee time" embroidered in white cursive down one sleeve. I remember the joy I'd felt finding the item in a Salvation Army store in Rocky Mount, North Carolina, during a spring-break service trip my senior year of college. My fellow volunteers and I browsed the store while covered in sweat and sawdust, badges of honor earned while building the frame of a house. We'd stopped to buy clean clothes on our way to shower at the YMCA before heading back to sleep on a gym floor with several dozen other college students. Holding that sweater, I could almost hear the snoring in the gym. Other items gave me joy because they had seemed like good deals, such as a giant, oversized brown corduroy shirt I'd bought for a quarter at a clothing sale at St. Michael's Church on the Navajo reservation. I had shirts from road races I'd run or from times when I remembered being happier, or feeling more sure of who I was. I look at each item. I pause. I decide to keep the memories and ditch the clothes.

I look at the open closet in front of me. Each item of clothing tells a story, and I wanted to keep those stories close to me. In keeping the clothes, I thought I could hang on to some part of who I was: thinner, freer, more creative. But I'm slowly realizing that I have other ways of expressing who I am. I still have my share of style quirks, but most items in my closet are now less shiny and more breathable. I don't need these things to remind me of who I was. As I begin taking the clothes off hangers and pulling them from bins, throwing them into piles on the floor, I feel lighter. Shedding these clothes is not getting rid of my old self, but freeing me to embrace who I am right now.

Here's what I get rid of the second time around:

- Three polo shirts
- One blouse (polyester, with blue and green flowers)
- Four sweaters
- Ten T-shirts, including the one I got when I joined the marsh-mallow Peeps fan club
- Three tank tops
- One pair of pajama pants
- Two shirts
- Four scarves
- Three pairs of dress pants, two of which were plaid
- Eight button-down shirts
- Six long-sleeved T-shirts
- Three skirts, one made of grey T-shirt material
- Two blazers, including one of white corduroy
- One denim trench coat
- Four tote bags
- One winter hat
- One purse
- One belt
- One jar opener grip

The total comes to fifty-nine items—fifty-nine more than I thought I could let go of when I started. And yet somehow it doesn't seem like enough. I send an e-mail to everyone I can think of to ask for their clothes, too. I know that sometimes the most difficult part about donating clothes is finding time to actually bring them down to the donation center, so I volunteer to pick them up from people. And they respond with enthusiasm.

I'm looking forward to returning to the Clothing Room with the new donations. My mind wanders back to the women I met there. At times they seemed to embody the diversity and chaos of the Clothing Room itself. And then they moved slowly toward the door, each woman holding on to her clothes in plastic bags, as though she was leaving any store in New York. Each woman grinning, or trying to muster something like it, and going her own way.

CHAPTER 11

—IN WHICH I IGNORE A HOMELESS MAN AND CONVERSE WITH A HOMELESS MAN

When I ran track during high school, my favorite event was the mile. I enjoyed how neat it was: four simple laps. The third lap was always the most difficult. In the first lap, you're still fresh; in the second and fourth, you've got adrenaline working in your favor. As you begin the third, you have the benefit of knowing you're halfway through, but you're suddenly exhausted and know that you still need to keep pace and then try to go even faster in the final lap. The third lap often made a difference between reaching my goal time or not. I keep this thought in mind as I settle into the third week of Lent. I sit down in my pew at St. Patrick's for morning Mass and reflect on how much already has happened that day.

I made it to the breadline again this morning. It was warm out for the first time, although it was still dark when I left my apartment. Don greeted me with a friendly hello and offered me a Danish. He said that he played the lotto, but it doesn't look like he won the jackpot. "One day I won't show up here, and you'll know I won," he said. Somehow I doubt that. Don's sense of service seems so sincere. I have a feeling he'd be back. Maybe he'd take a long vacation first, but he'd return in his Kansas City cap just as he has each day I've been here.

As I walked from the breadline on my way to Mass, a man standing by a deli asked if I could spare some change for his breakfast. I was caught off guard and muttered, "Sorry, sir," and looked away. It bothered me that the tall guy with the camel-hair coat was taking five sandwiches a day and this guy had none. It bothered me that I didn't react more charitably. If he'd been in the breadline, I would have smiled and said hello. And yet right down the street I found myself distancing myself from his reality. It is easy to compartmentalize life. To say: "This is when I deal with homeless people, this is when I feed the hungry, and then I am done." But at the heart of the Corporal Works of Mercy is making yourself available to those in need, even when it isn't convenient, even when you don't expect it. I need to recommit to this, I think. Despite Fr. Collins's Ash Wednesday warning to avoid Lenten list making, I'm getting too caught up in the tasks.

Yet it sometimes feels good to have a kind of Lenten routine: breadline, Mass, egg sandwich, office. I even find myself sitting in the same row at Mass, which happens to be behind the cute guy again. I'm embarrassingly conscious that I'm wearing the exact same outfit I had on the last time I saw him, although I'm also conscious of the fact that I know he doesn't remember that detail, or me.

During Mass, the priest begins the homily by saying, "We're halfway through Lent," and I sit up a little straighter. "It's a good time to look at how we're doing and see what we can do better so we don't end up in the same place we started." The priest goes on to quote a sermon from St. Peter Chrysologus, a fifth-century bishop:

"There are three things, my brethren, by which faith stands firm, devotion remains constant, and virtue endures. They are prayer, fasting, and mercy. Prayer knocks at the door, fasting obtains, mercy receives. Prayer, mercy, and fasting: these three are one, and they give life to each other."

The rest of the sermon reads, in part:

When you fast, see the fasting of others. If you want God to know that you are hungry, know that another is hungry. If you hope for mercy, show mercy. If you look for kindness, show kindness. If you want to receive, give. If you ask for yourself what you deny to others, your asking is a mockery.

Let this be the pattern for all men when they practice mercy: show mercy to others in the same way, with the same generosity, with the same promptness, as you want others to show mercy to you. . . .

Fasting bears no fruit unless it is watered by mercy. Fasting dries up when mercy dries up. Mercy is to fasting as rain is to earth. However much you may cultivate your heart, clear the soil of your nature, root out vices, sow virtues, if you do not release the springs of mercy, your fasting will bear no fruit.

When you fast, if your mercy is thin, your harvest will be thin; when you fast, what you pour out in mercy overflows into your barn. Therefore, do not lose by saving, but gather in by scattering. Give to the poor, and you give to yourself. You will not be allowed to keep what you have refused to give to others.

If anything will make me feel guilty about not running back to the breadline to grab a sandwich for the man on the corner, this is it. Take stock of the day, the priest says. It seems appropriate that I would receive this reminder just after realizing the need to reassess.

How *was* it going so far? I am still worried that I won't be able to do the remaining works of mercy, in particular "visit the sick" and "bury the dead." I've written to hospitals and parishes, but many volunteer programs in these areas require extensive training, vetting, or orientations. I've contacted Hart Island, the potter's field of New York, where the nameless dead are buried in graves dug by Rikers Island inmates. I have not heard back. I'm still trying to solidify my plans to visit San Quentin. I am worried about getting things done, which isn't really the point of Lent.

Later that afternoon, I head out of my office at lunch on my way to the drugstore. I pass the homeless man who almost always sits on a crate against the brick wall of the fast-food burrito shop next door. We exchange nods of vague recognition; I pass by him often, occasionally offering a dollar. He smiles and asks if I can spare some change, adding, "Hey, how ya doing today?"

"Good," I say. "I'll get you on the way back." As I leave the store, I pull out a dollar and keep it in my pocket, and as I pass the man again, I hand it to him. He nods, says thanks, and smiles. I start to continue on and then, for the first time, I stop in my tracks. I see myself passing by the other man near the breadline this morning. I remember the parable of Lazarus and the rich man, and I picture the rich man asking if he can warn me, even though I already have been told exactly what I need to do.

"I'm Kerry," I say, holding out my hand. "What's your name?" He looks surprised and then replies, "I'm Leroy; everyone knows me." And then, after a pause: "You work for the paper in there right?" Now it's my turn to be surprised. He sees me coming and going from the building, so I guess it makes sense.

"How's Fr. Drew? I haven't seen him out here for a while." Again, I'm surprised. He knows my boss by name. And not only that, but he cares how he's doing. "He's good," I say. "He had a cold, but he's recovering."

"Good, good. Tell him I say hello," Leroy says.

I'd walked by Leroy almost every day, but I'd failed to see him as a person. As I return to my desk, I hear the priest's words from the morning homily: what am I failing to do? Lately I've been focusing on what tasks I'm completing, but maybe I need to take a closer look at *how* I'm completing them. The enthusiasm of the first weeks has worn off a bit. I have been worried that this process was starting to empty me out, to leave me more emotionally or spiritually drained than when I began. But perhaps I have been expecting too much too soon. (The world probably looked pretty bleak to the apostles on the Saturday after Christ's crucifixion.) Maybe this process isn't leaving a void but a space that allows me to be filled with a new perspective, with a greater kind of love. God's mercy works in strange ways. I don't know where this process will lead me, but it's becoming clear that wherever I end up, I won't be the same.

CHAPTER 12

—IN WHICH I CONTEMPLATE THE RULES FOR RIDING THE SUBWAY

There are many rules regarding riding the New York City subway. Some are announced through tinny recordings—"A crowded train is no excuse for unlawful sexual contact." Others are shouted at passengers by frustrated train conductors—"Let 'em off! There's another train right behind this one"—as hordes of people push into the cars before other riders can get out. But other rules are tacit: "Always sit at least one seat away from everyone else if possible." "Don't make eye contact." Part of this code has developed, I think, because if you spend a good portion of your early morning crushed into a metal box full of strangers, then sometimes the only way to cope is to pretend they're not there. The result, however, is that you never really see any of them.

With so many people on board, you have to actively avoid eye contact by thumbing through a book, or playing a game on your phone, or wearing earbuds and closing your eyes to drown out the rumble of the train. Because once you make contact, there is nowhere for you to go; you've acknowledged one another as persons. Once you look people in the eye, it's harder to forget that they're human, that they're struggling, that God loves the man who just stepped on your foot and didn't apologize or the woman who shoved her way onto an already crowded train at the last second—God loves that person just as much as God loves you. God loves the man walking through the train cars with his hat held out in his hand, even as that person invokes God's name in an effort to shake you down for a dollar. Dorothy Day once said, "I really only love God as much as the person I love the least." What a terrifying prospect.

Lately, however, I find myself breaking one of these rules. More often I find myself looking up from the ground and looking into the faces around me, and seeing each person on the subway or on the street as someone's child. I'm not even sure why—perhaps since more of my friends are having babies—but I imagine that at some point a mother somewhere was in labor for hours and welcomed a child into loving arms, or maybe she worried about how she would manage to care for this child, or maybe she felt apathetic and didn't know why. And I imagine that deep down most of these women wanted the best lives possible for these children, and maybe they tried or maybe they didn't and life happened, and now here is her son, pulling metro cards out of a trash can, or with a down vest draped on his shoulders in the middle of summer, stumbling from one side of the train car to another. This method of seeing people has backfired, however, as I have even more trouble looking people in the eyes once my own begin to tear up.

And when I think of scenarios like these, I feel bad for feeling a bit overwhelmed in my own life. And yet, I am: the Corporal Works of Mercy seem mired in bureaucracy. It remains difficult to find someone sick to visit, and my search is starting to sound callous. I haven't been able to get up early enough to make it to the breadline for several days. I have some freelance writing that needs finishing. The cemetery has yet to get back to me about a possible visit with a gravedigger, and I'm worried I won't get a chance to bury the dead.

Some friends have suggested possible shortcuts. One went so far as to suggest that, were he to be taken out by the mob—or perhaps a more likely scenario in his neighborhood, by an angry hipster—he could actually be doing me some good, so long as he was still alive when I arrived on the scene. "Then, you can visit the sick, clothe the naked (this sounds wrong for some reason), ransom a captive, comfort the afflicted, *and* pray for the sick and dead. Wow, think of how many mercies you can hit," he wrote. I appreciated the support, but demurred; although I also acknowledged that the process he suggested sounded easier than getting up at 5:30 a.m. for the breadline. And while not everyone made such chivalrous gestures, I've been grateful for my friends' support across the board. So far, nearly a dozen friends have asked me to take their clothes or offered to bring them down themselves to the Clothing Room, and I now have several garbage bags filled with clothes lining the hallway of my apartment.

Still, the closest I'd come to visiting the sick was the time I stood near the door of the regional rail car, patting my friend on the back as she vomited into a plastic bag on our way home from a retreat. I stood in front of the little window of the door that looked back into the passenger area and could see people grimacing. One man dared approach us. I steeled myself, preparing to tell him to leave her alone, but he just smiled kindly and wordlessly handed us a sturdier plastic bag and a bottle of water. Quietly, humbly, *he* visited the sick and gave drink to the thirsty. And maybe that's the important thing about mercy, to respond in the best way you can right where you are.

It feels as if this whole Lenten season is rushing by all too quickly, and that I'll never have time to complete everything that needs to get done before Easter. But maybe that is part of the mystery of Lent: it takes us through Christ's suffering with him, so that we too might begin to do our Father's work. That we too might start to do work that may be difficult or misunderstood, work that we might never see finished. And yet, it is also work that may be surprising, that may give rise to new life we never expected.

CHAPTER 13

—IN WHICH I CONSIDER THE MEANING OF HOSPITALITY AND HOMELESSNESS

One of the best qualities of my friends is that they frequently remind me not to take myself too seriously. They do not let me get away with anything. They make me rethink things. Often this is through mockery, but encouraging mockery. I am chatting on the phone to a friend one night and mention that I have been stressing out. She asks which work of mercy I'm trying next. Shelter the homeless, I tell her. She wonders if that means I am taking people into my house. I tell her no, that I'm volunteering overnight at a homeless shelter. "So you're staying with *them*?" she laughs at the backward nature of the task. I can't say I hadn't seen the irony myself. Another friend peppered me with questions, as well:

"Will there be a locker to lock up your stuff?" I don't know.

"Will there be a separate room for you to sleep in?" I don't think so.

"Are you taking up a bed a homeless person could have?" Not that I know of.

I have never been truly homeless in the sense that I had nowhere to go, no one to take me in. However, for a few months after finishing graduate school I was without a place to call my own. I'd been hired for a temporary reporting job in Greenwich, Connecticut, where I was paid ten dollars an hour. This was not a feasible long-term option, but the job was interesting and my coworkers were kind, so I figured it was worth a shot. But living in the famously wealthy town of Greenwich on ten dollars an hour is (surprise!) pretty tough, and because I knew I wasn't staying there in the long term, getting an apartment in town wasn't affordable or practical.

A friend took pity on me and mentioned that her fiancé's parents would be out of town for some of that time, so I did some house sitting. When they returned, I stayed for several more days, and we occasionally had our own odd but awesome family dinners together before they moved, for good, to Seattle. Much as I tried to convince them to convince the new homeowners to keep me on as a quiet boarder upstairs, I eventually left when they did and headed for the couch of a friend in New Rochelle, New York, before finishing out my three months of couch surfing with friends in two separate apartments in the Bronx. During that time, I relied largely on what I began calling my "car-loset"—a combination car and closet—to store the majority of my clothes and the necessary belongings for the summer. My dad cut a metal rod that just fit between the handles bolted to opposite sides of the ceiling in the backseat of my red 1993 Camry. This is where I hung my clothes. This was a very convenient option if I needed to change before heading from work to dinner, but less convenient if I wanted to see out of the rear window.

As part of my reporting job, I drove my car-loset to local homes to take photos for the paper's real estate section and a feature called "Home of the Week." Stepping out of my car, I'd approach literal mansions and take photos of pools with fountains, kitchens with marble countertops, home theaters, and lakefront views. And then I'd return to my car—the only space I had that was my own at the time, which featured far fewer marble surfaces and exactly zero home entertainment features, unless you counted audiobooks on CDs.

A few years later, when I finally got my own place in New York, I searched for a one-bedroom so that I could be sure to offer visitors free rein over the living room if anyone wanted to stay with me. I made up my mind to have a kind of open-door policy. The rules are basically this: 1) Do you want to stay with me? Come on over. 2) Do you have a cousin's brother's sister-in-law who needs a place to crash? Here are my keys. I can't pretend to know what it's like to be truly homeless, but I do know what it's like to just need a place to call home for a little while.

This philosophy has sometimes resulted in somewhat unusual houseguests. I have housed a range of people, including a potentially violent friend with schizophrenia (a fact realized too late) and a complete stranger who was an acquaintance of my brother, and that stranger's sister. This particular pair happened to visit during a weekend when the old-fashioned glass dome of the light fixture in my bathroom inexplicably filled with water from the apartment above, necessitating that I refrain from using the bathroom light for two days while it dried out, as I had a strong (and possibly irrational) fear of starting an electrical fire via the damaged wires. It was a brutally hot summer night, and as I handed my guests a flashlight and wished them good luck as they went to brush their teeth, I think they wished they'd sprung for a hostel.

But this sort of hospitality presents surprisingly positive situations as well. Inevitably, I end up sitting around talking, in a way that's only possible while sitting together and sipping tea late into the night. In what is one of the most powerful passages in Dorothy Day's autobiography, *The Long Loneliness*, she speaks of the wonderful evolution of the Catholic Worker ministry, and writes about how many surprising, God-filled moments came about while "we were just sitting there talking." She writes of people moving in and out of the house and says, "Somehow the walls expanded." I can't help but think that here, she writes not only of the willingness of the community to take on and take in guests, but also of the walls of the heart growing in kind.

Because that is how our hearts are meant to work: just when you think your heart is full to the point of breaking, it adapts and grows and learns to love more than you ever thought you could. At least I hoped that was the case, because as I arrived at the Hurtado Shelter at Xavier, the reality of my situation hit me: I, a single, twenty-nine-year-old woman, plan to spend the night locked in a church basement with more than a dozen men I've never met. It's not that I don't trust them or that I think I'm in danger. It is, perhaps, just this element of the unknown. I have no idea what to expect.

CHAPTER 14

—IN WHICH I AM MISTAKEN FOR SPICY INDIAN FOOD

I arrive at the red-orange metal door of the shelter on 16th Street at the same time as Paul, my fellow volunteer, who is wearing a blue-checked shirt.

"The guys come around 8:00 p.m.," he tells me as he unlocks the door and leads me inside. The Hurtado Shelter, as it is known, feels strangely similar to the kind of place in which I would have attended a Brownie sleepover as a child, but with rough, folded cots instead of thin, Minnie Mouse–themed sleeping bags on the floor. The walls of the shelter are white, and the room is long and sparse. The cots are folded and lined up near the walls; each already has blankets on it. Near each bed are hooks on the walls, upon which to hang random personal items, presumably owned by the men: a few jackets, a suit coat on one hook; a plastic, gold-colored centurion helmet on another. One hook holds some felt reindeer antlers. Several have colorful plastic leis.

Paul shows me around. "The guys usually have their own beds; they know which ones are theirs. And if there's a new guy, they'll help him sort it out." We walk into the kitchen. There is a microwave sitting on the counter that appears to be the sort that is meant to be mounted under a cabinet. Along the right is a fridge and large, clear plastic drawers with labels. One is filled almost entirely with sugar packets. Another is labeled "oatmeal" but contains only boxes of raisins. To the left are more drawers with Styrofoam plates and bowls. The fridge has some cold cuts and several half-opened loaves of bread as well as individual tiny plastic containers of what appears to be salad dressing but which I later realize is peanut butter. The bottom two drawers are clear and filled with pats of butter, the kind in the plastic squares with the gold peel-off tops.

Paul hands me some grape juice to put on the table next to a giant silver bin of pears, which appears to be leaking. He then shows me the logbook, in which the volunteers record any incidents. "All quiet," most nights say. It reminds me of my days as a resident assistant in college.

We put out some bread and cold cuts and peanut butter and a basket of raisins from the oatmeal drawer. As I do this, it is slowly registering that this place is my home for the next few hours. The bed looks uninviting. I am washing my hands in the bathroom as I hear the sounds of metal legs of the beds smashing against the floor. The men have arrived. Someone knocks loudly on the door, and I try to make a quick exit, drying my hands on my denim skirt, which I'm wearing with a flowered cardigan.

A young man smiles broadly at me as I walk out and introduces himself as Angelo. He holds out his hand to shake mine. "Don't worry, they're clean," he says. I am not worried about germs, just shocked that he is so young. He couldn't be older than his early twenties. It reminds me of the time when I was a little girl and went with my mother to help at a soup kitchen. A young girl was celebrating her birthday there. She was about my age, and it struck me how similar and how far apart our lives were.

I look around as the guys settle in. One man with a red face and a black ponytail looks upset. He tries to speak Spanish to a man sitting on one of the beds and wearing a green-and-blue-plaid flannel shirt, but when the man in flannel doesn't respond, the man with the pony-tail switches to English. They must notice me watching them, because the man with the ponytail looks at me and says, "This is a good guy," pointing to the man in flannel. Another man, with glasses and wavy hair, speaks up in order to agree: "If he were to try to jump off the Empire State Building, I'd try to pull him back," he says. The man in flannel accepts this praise in silence.

Moments later, Angelo emerges from the bathroom. He almost immediately lies down in bed and crawls under a sheet and seems to be playing a video on a smartphone.

Paul introduces me to a man named Louis.

"This is Kerry," Paul says.

"Like the chicken," says Louis. I look confused for a moment.

Ah, *curry.*

Paul repeats my name, emphasizing the "e."

"Ah, like the movie," Louis says, unknowingly echoing Don, who weeks ago used the same horror film to establish my name in memory. I am suddenly concerned I am constantly giving off the wrong impression.

Next, Greg comes over. He is wearing a blue-grey sweatshirt and has several tattoos. "You could do a study on sleep apnea just in this room," he says with a laugh. We begin chatting, and the subjects range from our favorite kinds of chicken to the fact that he's been to Spring-field, Massachusetts, where I grew up.

Perry enters, just coming from work, a fact that surprises me. In fact, several of the guys have jobs and just can't make ends meet. "Can I go out a minute?" Perry asks Paul. Technically the men are supposed to stay inside the building for the rest of the night. "This guy gave me a meal last time and now I want to get him something." He approaches the man with the ponytail and asks if he wants anything. Ponytail says no thanks.

I ask Perry what he does for work. "I don't say around here," he says, pulling at his ear. "Everyone's listening." I don't ask anything else.

Greg tells me he has been all over New England and the Midwest. His dad was in the navy. When he finds out I work for a Jesuit magazine, he says he knew a guy who went to a Jesuit high school. As he talks, he spreads peanut butter on the toasted heel of bread and then rolls it up. "Are the Jesuits like the brothers up by St. Francis? Is there a rivalry, like gangs?" he asks, laughing. "Like the Sharks and the Jets," I say. "Lots of finger snapping."

Johnny, who has been sitting nearby, gets up and walks away and then comes back with a card that reads "St. Padre Pío House." He says it's at 155th Street in the South Bronx. "He was a priest who bled from his hands and feet," he says with a sweet pride at being able to connect my world to his. "Yeah, that's the stigmata," I say. Johnny nods.

Louis asks if I brought earplugs. I tell him no.

"I hope you're a good sleeper." He smiles knowingly.

A man wearing the uniform of a pizza shop employee stops by the table where we are seated. "Ugh," he says, "I'm a mess."

"You just wash your hands and face and it works wonders," Greg advises.

The man from the pizza restaurant tells us that his customers tell him jokes and then he gives them two free garlic knots, and then they come back and buy more pizza and his manager loves it. "What is the best joke you've heard?" I ask. "I forget," he says. Then he pauses; his face brightens. "The other day a girl says to me, 'What did the baby corn say to the mommy corn?' I give up. 'Where's pop corn?'" He smiles and heads off to wash his face.

Greg chimes in, "You have to let her think we're high-quality home-less people," he says and laughs. And until that moment, I hadn't realized that, deep in conversation, I'd forgotten about that label for a while. I hadn't tried to categorize the men as crazy or Christ-like. I'd just let them be. And I'd allowed myself to be present.

Meanwhile, off to one side, Johnny has set up a metal folding chair as a kind of bedside table. He places a bowl on it, alongside an inhaler, a cracked hand mirror, a toothbrush, and other toiletries. "You staying over?" he asks. I say yes. He shrugs. "I guess we're not walking around in our skivvies tonight," he replies. "It's a pain to have to get dressed to go to the bathroom." I feel bad that I've inconvenienced him, but I appreciate his consideration. More than ever, I feel like I am their guest.

As the evening continues, some men head to bed early, and others watch TV. Paul turns to me and says, "Is this what you expected?" I have to admit it's not, though I can't say exactly what I thought it would be like.

"Most of these guys, if you met them outside of here, you wouldn't know they were homeless," Paul says. "They say that this shelter is one of the nicer ones."

Even so, my sheets have stains on them. I ask Paul if I can get new sheets, and he tells me to check the back hall. There are stacks of white, scratchy sheets, all flat sheets, and all are stamped with the words "Property of Dept. of Homeless Services" in purple ink. I grab two and carry them back to my bed, which is tucked into an alcove several feet from Paul's and separated by a nightstand in the center. We chat about publishing and my sister's upcoming wedding as the men settle into their own beds, which line the perimeter of the room.

Finally, Paul shuts out the light around 10:30. I have a difficult time falling asleep. Around 11:00, one of the guys' phones rings. It seems that everyone is snoring, and I understand now why Louis asked me about the earplugs. The snoring is at all volume levels and intervals, so at times it sounds almost like one continuous rumble. A guy starts hacking. Someone brushes off his sheets. And yet somehow, after talking with a lot of the guys that evening, all the noise doesn't really bother me. I'm grateful for their welcome. Throughout the evening, the place seemed to grow larger, as the men made sandwiches or watched movies or just sat there talking. I feel surprisingly at home.

CHAPTER 15

—IN WHICH I ATTEND THE STATIONS OF THE CROSS

As I awake to the clanking of beds being refolded and placed against the walls, and the shuffle of bags and clothes and cleaning, it strikes me what a luxury it is to be able to decide when I get up each morning. To have the option to spend a day in bed with a book or to rest at home watching some sort of TV marathon. To have a place where I am able to stay or go as I please. But the guys have to be out of the house by 6:30 a.m., so I quickly get up at 5:30, as well, as they prepare for their day. I have slept in all of my clothes, so it does not take me long to get ready. I smooth out my cardigan and begin to sweep the floor and wipe down the bathroom. The fluorescent lights feel especially harsh this morning. The men get ready quickly and relatively quietly, and they're out the door soon and nearly all at once. I wave good-bye as they head out to board their bus. I thank them and thank Paul, and then I'm out the door, too, back onto 16th Street outside the shelter. Even though it's a familiar street, I'm disoriented by the unfamiliar timing and the fact that it's still dark. I contemplate heading home but decide the best thing to do is to head straight to work, where I change and wash my face in the office bathroom, much as the guys had done at the shelter.

I fuel my work hours with a few cups of coffee, push through the day, and later that evening I find myself on a rush-hour subway ride back to 16th Street, where I pass by the shelter again on my way to attend the stations of the cross at St. Francis Xavier parish. The stations of the cross is a devotion based on the events that precede Jesus' crucifixion and resurrection, often described as the Passion. These events are at the core of the Christian faith. Often the faithful walk together through a church while meditating on artistic representations of the events and listening to readings and song. This devotion allows one to consider these events in a deliberate and meaningful way, within the context of a church community. Which is why I feel guilty about dreading it. In the past my mind frequently has wandered as I've walked from station to station, trying to use the repetitive nature of the hymns and prayers like a mantra.

My friend Tim, whom I have known since high school, volunteered to accompany me, and I quickly took him up on the offer. I enter the gorgeous, old church, with its high ceilings and cream-colored walls. I sit on the left side, about halfway up. I've attended Mass here frequently, but I'm not usually in the church at night, and I appreciate the new perspective and warm glow. From my seat, I take the time to really look around in a way I don't usually do when I rush in on Sunday mornings. A giant, circular mural looks down on me from the center of the ceiling. The crowd is smaller than the Sunday morning one, but it's not bad considering it's a Friday night in New York. The thing I love about many New York churches is that their physical location is deeply embedded in the city, spires sticking up between coffee shops and high-rise apartment buildings, their statues of Mary on corners beside chic restaurants or the gaudy awnings of bodegas. Their locations seem to represent exactly where the church, as a whole, is meant to be: at the heart of people's lives, visible, integrated, and with open doors.

I leaf through the archdiocesan newspaper as I wait for Tim to arrive. I think about my sister, who took part in many a Passion play during grade school. She and the other student actors worked for weeks to perfect their performances and memorize lengthy monologues. One year, my sister Elizabeth was assigned the part of the unrepentant criminal, one of two men who hung on the cross next to Christ as he died. (The other asked for Jesus' forgiveness.) I still recall her powerful delivery: "I wanted to live a little longer, but [Jesus] seemed to welcome death as if it were a door to a greater life," she said in character.

I was impressed by her performance and moved by the message, but even such a lively production failed to instill in me an ongoing love for the stations of the cross. I know that the story of the passion of Christ should be at the heart of everything I do, all that I have based my life around, and yet, somehow, I can rarely bring myself to sit through all fourteen stations. Too often I grow tired of the repetition, of moving slowly, of feeling like I'm barely making progress as I count down to the final station. For some reason, it doesn't feel productive.

Like the production my sister participated in, these stations are creative and inclusive. The first reading is from Mark, chapter 26, in which Jesus goes out to pray in the garden and the disciples are meant to stay awake and watch. Instead, they fall asleep. "Could you not stay awake with me one hour?" Jesus asks Peter. Having just attempted to peruse the program to estimate how long these stations might take, I feel as though these words are directed to me. So I let go. I agree to stay awake for the hour or two that these might take, and—not just physically, but spiritually—to stay vigilant, to listen, and to be present.

The parish bell choir offers a beautiful rendition of the hymn "Stay with Me." At each station, someone from one of the various ministries within the parish offers a brief reflection in addition to the Scripture reading. The person from the abilities ministry speaks at the second station, praying for those with health concerns and encouraging the sick to persevere with grace and dignity.

Many of the songs and hymns of this service are so ingrained in my Lenten experience, I realize that, too often, I am not actually listening to the words I am singing or saying. We sing, "Jesus, remember me, when you come into your kingdom." I think about my sister's monologue, and the criminals crucified beside Christ, and the choice that we all have to be the kind of people who ask for forgiveness or who refuse to do so. How many times do I say, with my actions or with my inattention to prayer, *I don't need you, God*, the way the unrepentant criminal did, and yet still expect to be treated like the repentant one? *I don't have time for you, God, but hey, remember* me *anyway*. But the thing is, God does. God remembers me. Every day. Even when I don't deserve it, and perhaps especially when I don't deserve it.

The crowd moves to each station, but it's large enough that by the time the fifth station rolls around, the congregation has spread out a bit. Some people are in the pews, some in the middle aisle, some are around the back of the pews, but no one is too far, and we're all focused on the same thing. It feels like a real community, standing here, staying awake together.

At the sixth station, we hear the legend of Veronica, who is said to have wiped the face of Jesus as he carried his cross, and then the speaker reads the passage from the Gospel of Matthew, which describes the Works of Mercy. Tim looks over his shoulder at me and taps the program, as if to say, "Pay attention; they're talking about those things that you're trying to do." In the reflection that follows, the reader says, "Sometimes all we can do is wipe the sweat from someone's brow as they suffer."

By the time we reach the twelfth station, I realize that time has gone by much faster than I thought it would. Already we are all standing in front of a life-size image of Christ on the cross. For most of my life, the stations in churches I've visited have been small paintings or wall carvings placed at intervals, but at Xavier they're much larger panels, and I find myself connecting with the scenes in a new way. In the spirit of St. Ignatius, I imagine all of us as extensions of the image before us, truly present at the foot of the cross, standing beside those depicted in the scene, wondering what it means and what is in store. We are all at different places in our journeys, but united somehow, true companions. The stations of the cross no longer seem like boring repetition but like something closer to a journey. Perhaps what's always frustrated me about the stations is that they cut too close to some of the struggles in my own spiritual life: the desire to keep moving forward rather than be still; the desire to skip the process and try to jump straight to the end, to that resurrection moment, where we get to celebrate; the desire to ignore or avoid the suffering along the way.

At the fourteenth station, the image of Jesus being placed in the tomb, my eyes are drawn up, to a separate image high above the stations. It is one of dozens of people being crucified, stretched out along a road toward the horizon. It is the first time I've noticed it, as I rarely stand in this part of the church. The juxtaposition of these images is striking. As Christ is being taken down from the cross, below, in the image above, those who have chosen to follow him continue to suffer. They are taking up his work, taking on the cross. And as we stand there, our own group is included in that tradition, all of us part of a long line of people in love with, pained by, suffering for, and taking part in the church. There can be a strange beauty in suffering, but, more important, there is beauty in having a community that helps us overcome it, to move forward toward that resurrection.

When I began attending the RCIA sessions, Fr. Collins asked each of us to draw an image that represented what the church meant to us. I drew a three-ring circus, with a stick-figure ringmaster, a trapeze artist, and a tiger that looked more like a striped house cat. And though I knew it was unusual, I drew it not out of mockery but because I felt that Catholicism, at its best, invites everyone to come together—even people society might view as freaks—each with his or her unique talents, sometimes taking risks, sometimes looking like fools, underneath the big tent of the church. Fr. Collins's own drawing was simpler. Two lines ran vertically down the length of the paper toward the horizon. Throughout he'd drawn simple circular faces of different sizes and colors. Some had smiles, others had frowns, and some had straight, slanty mouths. Some were along the margins and others were right in the center. It was the view, he said, from one moment at Mass when he'd been on the altar, looking out toward the congregation. And he saw two new Catholics come forward to receive the Eucharist, joining the communion lines streaming toward him, all with their own expressions of faith, all at different places in their journeys. And looking at that scene made him see beyond the people in front of him to all those who'd come before, and all those who would follow.

The bell choir rings out a final version of "Stay with Me." As I sing along, the words become not simply a request from Christ, but *of* Christ. Because, Lord knows, I can't do this alone.

CHAPTER 16

—IN WHICH I SPEND ST. PATRICK'S DAY SURROUNDED BY WATER

I am holding tightly to the metal handrail in the subway car when a man gets on and begins screaming about salvation. This is not unusual. "Ladies and gentlemen," he says, "even if you feed all the homeless people it doesn't mean you're going to heaven. You are only saved through Jesus Christ; his blood was poured out on that cross to atone for our sins." He continues with a stump speech that adds a bit of fire and brimstone, gaining volume as he sees the passengers following the unspoken subway rules and keeping their eyes on the floor. This is the standard New York response to transit evangelists.

Then, suddenly, a woman breaks protocol and looks up. "So," she says directly, "what's your point?"

The man doesn't skip a beat as he recycles lines from the speech in response. "No," she says, flatly rejecting his theory. "You can't live a life of sin and then just say you believe in Jesus and end up in heaven. It's based on how you live your life."

The subway evangelist clearly isn't used to receiving this much attention, and it's hard to tell if he's thrilled or annoyed. But he's also run out of responses, so he turns away and walks through the doors at the end, taking his eschatology to the neighboring car.

A short time later, I emerge from the subway on the Upper West Side. I dodge small drunken crowds of college students as I make my way toward the Cathedral of St. John the Divine, the largest Episcopal church in the city. It is St. Patrick's Day, and tiny, sparkly green hats seem to be a popular choice among this year's revelers. I'm slightly more subdued, sporting a green jacket as I head toward the steps of the imposing grey gothic structure. The church is currently showing an exhibit about the value of water called, appropriately, "The Value of Water." I figured understanding this would be helpful in my quest to give drink to the thirsty.

On my way to the church, I'd passed an old pay-phone station with a large ad on the side from NYC Environmental Protection: a grey and green bird held a glass in his wing. Beneath him were the words: "Drink Tap Water." Below that was a little blurb: "NYC has some of the best water in the world. It travels to us from pristine reservoirs in the Catskill Mountains. Mmmm . . ."

Closer to the church, the signs became a bit more philosophical. The fences surrounding the churchyard sported blue banners with quotes about the meaning of water from sources as diverse as Toni Morrison, Confucius, Van Gogh, the Qur'an, and the Gospel of John. The quote from John is from the King James Bible, which sounds almost foreign to me: "He that believeth on me, as the scripture hath said, out of his belly shall flow rivers of living water." The verse paints a strange picture of a possibility that, frankly, seems less than desirable when taken at face value.

I enter the church and get a ticket for the tour. Thus far I'm the only one waiting, which doesn't surprise me, given that water is not exactly the liquid most associated with St. Patrick's Day. Eventually I am joined by a man in khaki pants and a green shirt and two women also dressed in earth tones.

Our tour guide arrives in a teal sundress, knit scarf, southwestern print sweater, and brown boots. The guide, like me, seems to be in her twenties, but everyone else appears to be in their sixties. The guide leads us to the first installation in which a black outline of a rowboat tied to a post is projected onto a stone wall. The boat is bobbing along the stone, but there are no lines to indicate water.

Our tour guide gathers our small group and asks us what's missing. She seems to want to make this a discussion, but my fellow tour mates are resisting. There's an awkward silence. "Um, water." I say. "Right," she says, looking both grateful and annoyed. "You're supposed to be thinking about water, but it's not shown to us. Where the water should be is a void; it is nothing; it is not there," she continues with some dramatic flair. "It's an indication of the attention we need to pay to it."

The next work consists of plastic bottles cut into spirals and combined with yarn and wire into a sort of waterfall. "What can you find?" the guide asks. "Plastic bottles, yarn, and wire" seems too obvious an answer, so I search the scene to figure out what the guide is looking for, but she gives us a look and mutters, "No? OK." And our reticent group shifts to the next stop.

This one features large strips of plastic flowing down from umbrella-like domes, all lit in an eerie fashion, as though a jellyfish made of trash has been hanged. The guide looks at us expectantly. Then, after a moment, one of the earth-tone women breaks the silence: "Why don't you tell us?"

"It looks like this fountain of light but really it's made of trash, which is something that is choking our rivers and world," the guide says without cheer. As the tour continues, everyone seems to mellow out a bit. I am fascinated by the various images and interpretations of what water is, what it can be, and what it represents.

We reach a small chapel in which glass jugs line a high ledge encircling the room. Each one has the name of a country and an amount written on it. Our guide offers some context, telling us that the basic water requirement for a person is 50 liters a day. The numbers on each jug represent what people actually use. Canada listed 818 liters, with the United States claiming 598 per person. At the opposite end of the spectrum was Somalia, with less than 8 liters. Even though my church and my city urge me to consider the use and impact of water, I realize that conservation is not something I think about as often as I should.

My own thoughts about water tended to bring to mind vacations and relaxation. I recalled a trip I took with some friends to the south of France during my junior year of college—how we spent an early morning sitting on a rock jetty letting the spray hit our faces and listening alternately to the sound of the waves and the sounds coming through our headphones. How in the afternoon we waded into the freezing water and contemplated what would happen if we just kept going and whether or not we could make it to Africa. How later that night we sat on the sand, and a tiny child beside us yelled, "La mer!" with such genuine enthusiasm. How I felt that the world was beautiful and I was beautiful because I was a part of it, which is not an insignificant feeling for a sometimes awkward twenty-year-old woman wearing a grey hooded sweatshirt and grubby sneakers. I had many lovely memories of water, but rarely had I feared that I wouldn't have enough to drink.

A few weeks ago at RCIA, Fr. Collins asked us to write down what we think of when we hear the word *water*. I wrote: tap water in NYC, the Rockaways, Lake Michigan, ice, glaciers, fire hydrants, swimming at Bass Pond, baptism, holy water, the Mediterranean. Then he asked us to write down properties of water. I wrote: cleansing, purifying, destroy, wear away, cool, calm, excite, quench/satisfy, assist with travel, nourish, drown, carry, give life.

Then we read the Gospel story of the woman at the well. Christ offers the waters of new life to her. Continuing the meditation on water, Fr. Collins said, "We are urged to ask ourselves, 'Where do I need this water, and for what?'"

I need water to live, to quench my thirst. I need water to cleanse myself. But we're talking about the life-giving waters, which may or may not come from one's belly. And it occurs to me that I often take these waters for granted as well, treating God as a kind of divine faucet that I expect to pour out grace on demand, but which I ignore when I'm not feeling thirsty, when I am busy trying to quench my thirst with things that are less refreshing or life-giving.

At the Crucifixion, the centurion pierced Jesus' side, and out poured blood and water, the Scriptures say. In this somewhat odd and graphic image it's clear this life-giving water goes hand in hand with suffering. If you want the water, you often have to take all that comes with it.

"Maybe I am a rock, and maybe I need water to deal with that," Fr. Collins offered in our meditation. "Do I need water like a glacier to grind me down? What we're asking is for God to give us the water we need. Why am I not letting the water in? How do I dismantle this dam? So we pray as the Samaritan woman did: 'How do I get this water?'"

CHAPTER 17

—IN WHICH I AVOID THRUSTING CUPS AT RUNNERS

It is just after five in the morning, and already I am speed walking across Central Park for the second time. Between the breadline, the homeless shelter, and this particular morning, I'm beginning to get the impression that one can do God's work only at ungodly hours.

I have been up since 4:00 a.m. in order to arrive at my race volunteer station by 5:00. I've made it to the park, but now I just need to find the table. I've been redirected by several kind but possibly pre-morning-coffee volunteer coordinators, which has resulted in my somewhat fast-paced scramble. The fourth week of Lent is just beginning, and I'm volunteering as a "fluid station" volunteer, which means I am handing out water to runners at the NYC Half marathon, which winds through Central Park.

After joining up with a couple of other confused volunteers wandering through the park, we come across our assigned fluid station, which at this point consists of a long row of folding tables and a few white paper cups. Behind the table, another volunteer coordinator is handing out reflective vests and lanyards with credentials—which I have to admit make me feel kind of cool and official—and free knit caps, which ease slightly the pain of the cold air that is cutting through the still, dark morning. Alongside the tables and the volunteers are several enormous plastic trash cans lined with clear plastic trash bags. One end of a hose hangs over the edge of one of the cans, filling it with water. It takes a minute for it to sink in that the other end is connected to a nearby fire hydrant. On the tables are clear plastic pitchers, the sort you see on the tables at family-style Italian restaurants with red-and-white-checked tablecloths. I think back to the ad I had seen the day before about NYC, with the bird and the cartoonishly drawn peaks of the Catskill mountain range and the claim that New York City has some of the best water in the world, and I hope the claim is correct.

Prior to my arrival, I'd received via e-mail nearly two pages of instructions regarding the logistics of volunteering at the fluid station. This text had included a warning that while handing out water and sports drinks "may seem like a simple function, it is far more difficult than it appears." The main point seemed to be that we should not get in the way of the runners. One line, written in bold and all caps, read: "Volunteers Should Not Thrust Cups At Runners Or Force Them On Runners." I tried to imagine what this would look like—perhaps grabbing a runner by the shirt and forcing a tiny paper cup into his hand. Or randomly jabbing my arm out into the sea of runners and clotheslining one of them. I felt confident that I was up to the task of not attacking people.

Some of the volunteers begin placing rows and rows of paper cups along the tables. I grab one of the clear pitchers and dunk it into the plastic-bag-lined trash can of hydrant water. I hold it up to try to catch the light. It looks clear enough, or at least clearer than the water from my old apartment in the Bronx, so I begin to pour. The key is to fill the cup only about a third of the way so that runners don't spill the fluid all over themselves while running but still have enough to quench their thirst. I pour and pour and pour, moving as quickly as I can through hundreds of cups. When we fill the table surface, a volunteer team captain comes by and places a piece of lightweight white poster board on top, and we begin to add more cups on top of it, creating a second layer, and then a third, a kind of paper-cup house of cards.

And then we wait. We talk about races we've run in the city, other volunteer opportunities, and how cold we are. And then, eventually, it grows light and the runners begin to arrive. The first to arrive are the long, lean, Kenyan runners, who don't seem to need to fuel up at this point in the race, and who breeze by effortlessly. I realize that for all the road races I've run, I've never actually seen the best runners at work, having always been stuffed in some corral at the starting line, hundreds of people behind. And then there's a gap, before the fastest of the regular folks come streaming through. I've always loved road races for their equality. There are few sports where professionals and amateurs alike can compete in the same competition, on the same grounds, exposed to the same elements, joys, and challenges.

The thing with handing out water is that you don't really have to hand it out. If runners want it, they'll swoop by the table and grab one. There's no danger of me clotheslining anyone. I simply move the cups up to the edge of the table replacing the ones taken so that runners don't need to reach as far. I know that my friend Tim will be among the runners, so I scan the crowd for him as the people stream past. Finally I see him, and I cheer as he dodges the crowd to make his way to my part of the fluid station. He's jogging in place and looking worried. "Can you call my mom? I was running really late and, in the rush to get to the starting line, locked my keys in the car before I got here, and I need her to call AAA to get them out." I agree. "Aren't you supposed to give me water?" He asks with his usual sarcasm. I reply in similar fashion and tell him to get it himself. He grabs a cup and is off running again. I pick up my cell phone to call his mother.

A few minutes later, most of the runners have gone past. And then it is over and there are probably a couple hundred cups left over. We are told to clean up, and we pause for a minute, looking over all the cups that remain, realizing what that means. The volunteer to my left grabs the edge of the folding table, and with a single motion pushes it forward toward the road. Water and cups cascade to the ground, settling into a soggy paper cloud on the blacktop. "And to think," she says, "people are without water in India and Kenya." I wonder how many jugs from the cathedral's art exhibit this would have filled up. How many people on earth are thinking, "How can we get this water?" We grab shovels and begin pushing the cups into trash bags and folding up the tables.

It occurs to me that not only have I not thrust a single cup at a runner, I have not actually handed out a single cup, just nudged them forward to put them within reach. I can't say it's the most useful I've ever felt. And yet there is something humbling about being available to people even if only for a moment; it's a strange sort of roadside hospitality.

I think back to the story of the woman at the well, to the sort of water she was offered. I imagine Jesus sending out a two-page memo to his disciples, saying, "I know this seems easy, but it's more complicated than it looks. And: Do Not Thrust This Water In The Pharisees' Faces." And sometimes we're like the woman from the water tour; we just want someone to tell us what it's all about, to explain to us what to think or how to respond. We want to look at God and say, "Why don't you tell us?"

This is part of the beauty of the faith, that these waters are offered, they're ready for us, ready to fill our thirst, but never forced on us. We have to choose when and how much and how often to drink, with Christ standing always along the course, nudging the cups toward us.

This is one of my favorite things about working with RCIA, seeing how thirsty people are for spiritual growth, how readily people like Lauren and Zubair and Jackie have arrived. I try to do my best to support them through the process. And sometimes all you can do is pour out as much water as you can, welcome people to the table, and cheer them on as they continue to run their own race.

CHAPTER 18

—IN WHICH I ATTEMPT TO CREATE A LENT-APPROPRIATE DATE

In the world of online dating you never know what will appeal to someone. His profile mentioned midnight Mass and the fact that he was educated by Jesuits, so I reached out. I got an e-mail back that same night. It mentioned food vendors and national parks, storytelling and British sitcoms. He said his mom knit blankets for the Pine Ridge Indian Reservation and, kindly, that I "seemed completely awesome." He suggested we go out for a drink.

It's rare to receive a response from a potential date that's interesting and creative and makes use of proper grammar. I found it was easy to respond with genuine interest, although I insisted that I was, at most, 96 percent awesome.

I'd be happy to join him for a drink, I wrote, except for the fact that I gave up alcohol and sweets for Lent. I realized this probably sounded ridiculous and I acknowledged as much in my e-mail response, mentioning that I'd normally enjoy a good whiskey and ginger ale, in hopes of softening the blow. I also mentioned the small matter that I was leaving shortly for a conference in California, and then, I hoped, prison. My plans for the visit seemed to be coming together.

I told him I would be happy to grab coffee or tea with him or to sit in a bar and drink soda (and then tip the server generously to make up for my lack of drinking). I let him know that I had literally one evening available before I left and that it might be easier just to wait until I returned. And then, still nervous about his reaction, I wrote: "Of course, it's possible that you're not interested in dating the type of person who gives up stuff for Lent. If that's the case, I completely understand. No worries, and no need to reply. Although, even if you've now lost interest, it sounds like I could totally be friends with your mom. She sounds lovely." I reread my e-mail and thought that maybe it's a wonder anyone ever responds to me at all.

I'd struggled with the best way to bring up my temporary life of prohibition with my potential dates. Replying in a straightforward way with attempts at humor had become standard. And I'd been surprised by the overwhelmingly positive reactions from most people. In fact, people often were interested to learn more and were more than happy to accommodate. There had been the guy who had not only suggested dinner, but dinner at a vegan restaurant,because although he himself was not Catholic, he knew that at some point during Lent Catholics didn't eat meat, and he wanted to make sure I had options. And there was the guy who ordered the fresh fruit for our shared dessert knowing that I couldn't eat sweets. Still, I tried to offer people the option of a graceful exit if the news of my Lenten observations made them want to run.

Adam didn't run. In fact, he wrote back to say that, while he had not given up alcohol for Lent, he had given up coffee. And soda. And all desserts. Naturally, I was delighted. And then perplexed. In our Lenten sacrifices we had eliminated two of New York's most popular dating options. I could have a coffee and he could have a drink, and we could see how long we each lasted without trying to steal a sip, but this seemed less than ideal. Adam went on to discuss the time he went to Per Se, one of New York's fanciest restaurants, on a Sunday during Lent, after he learned about the much-debated practice of "breaking

Lent" on Sundays. I wondered how many other people on the dating site were discussing such things.

We weighed our options, trying to find a place where neither of us would face too much temptation. "If all else fails, we could always get a head of lettuce and a couple of bottles of water and sit on a curb somewhere. That may be the only safe Lenten option for us both." I wrote helpfully. Because I'm a romantic.

Eventually, Adam suggested a restaurant that could only exist in New York: one that served only one meal. He sold me on it by writing, "Stodgy waitresses and steak frites?" Because he is a romantic too.

When Adam arrives, he is sporting a scruffy beard and a blue-green plaid coat. We talked about the Muppets and poetry, and I tried (at his request) and failed to recite my favorite poem, which is Joyce Carol Oates's "Night Driving." I got through most of it. But no one is impressed by people who remember *most* of poems. Still, I didn't feel a terrible need to impress, which is nice, and we got along well. He told me about his grandmother, who was suffering with dementia, and with whom he sometimes stayed up late at night, caring for her in her illness and making sure she was safe. We continued to chat as he walked me back to Grand Central, where I could grab the 7 train home. I considered the date a success, and we agreed to keep in touch while I was away.

Now, a few days later, driving up the California coast in my rented Ford, I felt a million miles away from the maze of people and cabs and streets around Grand Central. Rather, I felt like the road embodied the freedom of a Bruce Springsteen song, except instead of looking at the refinery fires of New Jersey, I was looking at the Pacific Ocean, which, much as I love the grit of the Garden State, was a marked improvement. I was headed from Los Angeles to San Francisco on a road that felt like it led to greatness simply because a road lined with such beauty could hardly lead otherwise.

My exchanges with the prison staff in San Quentin had finally pro-
duced results, and after a conference in Anaheim, I was on my way
to northern California to visit friends, a prison chaplain, and several inmates. I stayed overnight in Santa Barbara in an adorable bed-
and-breakfast that had left me an egg croissant sandwich in a basket.
I devoured the sandwich and managed to ignore the chocolate chip
cookies in the lobby.

Traveling by myself is, for the most part, exciting and empowering,
but there are moments when I wished I had someone alongside me.
The previous night I'd eaten an excellent salad at a restaurant bar facing the wall near the cash register and texted with Adam. Not exactly
as romantic as our first date.

It feels strange to be driving so close to the literal edge of the country. I pull off the road into small areas to take photos of the views. It's
so different from what I'm used to seeing every day in the city, so open
and peaceful. But city life has other advantages. There's beauty in New
York, too—in the architecture, in the diversity of the crowds, and in
the many gorgeous museums.

Of course there are days when everything seems to go wrong, and
at those times it is easy to turn your back on the city—or more accu-
rately, perhaps, to feel that it's turned its back on you. Months earlier
I'd felt this way after a difficult breakup. A part of me had longed to
get out of New York, which sometimes seems suffocatingly small. But
I was in Midtown at 7:30 p.m. on a Tuesday, and it seemed that the
more practical option was to rise above. As I wandered through Rockefeller Plaza, I noticed a small kiosk selling tickets to the Top of the
Rock, the roof of 30 Rockefeller Center. It was overpriced. It seemed
ridiculous. But it was also probably not too crowded. I bought a ticket
and walked into the lobby, up a huge winding staircase, through some
displays and a huge screen, and into the elevator. It had a clear ceiling and the elevator shaft was lined with red and blue lights. Images of

NBC television shows were projected overhead. It was tremendously cheesy and yet comforting.

The night was mild, and so the observation deck was not as cold as it might have been for a January night. I pushed my earbuds into my ears and hit play on my iTunes. The soundtrack from *The Muppets* began.

There is a great tradition in film of romance at the top of New York City skyscrapers. But as I looked out from 30 Rock toward the Empire State Building, lit with white lights, it was Kermit the Frog who came to mind. That scene from *The Muppets Take Manhattan,* in which, after failing to get his show on Broadway, Kermit climbs to the top of that building and screams to no one and to everyone: "I'm not giving up. I'm still here and I'm staying. You hear that New York? I'm staying here. The frog is staying." And so I looked out, feeling defiant, and only mildly foolish for finding encouragement in the words of a felt frog. I slowly walked around and absorbed the rest of the skyline, anonymous shapes against the dark soup of the sky. Then, suddenly, I recognized an office building—*his*—unassuming in its warm glow. I felt a sharp pain in my gut and took a deep breath. I didn't know why I hadn't expected this. And I saw the dozens of times I'd met him so many stories below, on our way to dinner or Central Park. Perched high above the city, I felt so very far from all of that. And I thought I might cry, but I did not. I had not yet cried. I just clenched my jaw and closed my eyes and stood very still.

I overheard the couple next to me talking. A man was pointing out buildings and bridges and boroughs. The woman responded in awe: "The city is just so big." I opened my eyes again. One of the man's arms was around the woman, the other reached out toward the darkness, the light. I squinted toward the office building. It no longer loomed so large. It just seemed like any one of the thousands of other structures lined up, fading into the black, a small piece of a vast landscape.

And I felt like I could see, too, everyone whose lives were framed in the tiny squares of light in front of me, dancing around each other in the uneasy rhythm of the city. The wind continued to blow, but the blackness of the sky felt warmer. Sometimes hope comes in the form of a million faces you have yet to meet. I took another deep breath and knew that there was so much life in front of me. I looked straight ahead and smiled. And through the jagged teeth of its skyline, the city seemed to grin back.

CHAPTER 19

—IN WHICH I GET INTO PRISON
IN CALIFORNIA, TWICE

In order to reach the hundreds of men who are cut off from the outside world, I must first drive down a street lined with quaint houses that feels very much a part of the outside world. The California homes are small but sweet, with pretty, if sometimes unruly, yards that look over misty San Francisco Bay. Now, in the fifth week of Lent, I direct the car over a short hill into a good-sized parking lot adjacent to a long, high fence that surrounds San Quentin State Prison, where I wait. I am early, as is my habit.

These few spare moments seem to be a good time to plug in my iPod and turn on an album I've downloaded specifically for this trip: *Johnny Cash Live at San Quentin*. I click ahead to the song "San Quentin." I lean back, and as Cash belts out "San Quentin, I hate every inch of you . . ." to a cheering throng of inmates, it all feels a bit meta. And a little badass.

From the driver's seat, I notice others getting out of their cars and walking toward the entrance to the prison. The whole place looks more like a kind of castle than a place for incarceration, and the main building has a seemingly out-of-place Tudor style. The few visitors I can see are mostly women who arrive one or two at a time. I wonder about the backstories of the visitors, and those inmates they

101

have come to see. Are they visiting a son, a brother, a boyfriend, a husband?

It's a striking contrast to Alcatraz, where tourists arrive by the boat-load, even in the rain, as I had done just the day before. There, entire families clamber onto the island to immerse themselves in the prison's history and the mystique of gangsters long gone. Today, there is little evidence that crowds are lining up to visit the prison filled with the living.

As I'd walked around Alcatraz, I was struck by the voices on the audio tour. They were voices of the real people who had lived and worked there—wardens and inmates and family members. It was moving to listen to their memories of the difficulties and challenges and even surprising joys of spending days and nights on this strange island, so close to San Francisco and yet so far.

While in line for the boat to Alcatraz, I had been asked to stand in front of a fake backdrop featuring a photo of the island in the distance to have my picture taken. The background had a sunny, blue sky, which contrasted with the grey, cold, rainy skies we were experiencing. I had no desire to capture my current look—cold and rain-soaked, and covered in a thin, overpriced plastic poncho purchased from the gift shop and snack area, so I politely declined.

As soon as I got off the boat, I was greeted by three signs on the main building, an old stone structure. One sign was the brown and green arrowhead of the National Park Service logo. Another said "United States Penitentiary," and listed several warnings, a remnant of its working days. The final sign was less official, simply featuring hand-painted red letters that read, "Indians Welcome," a remnant of the takeover of the island by Native American rights activists from 1969 to 1971. Together these signs sum up the strange incongruity of this prison.

Alcatraz is a place once filled with men who committed grave evils, and sometimes innocent ones who had been wronged. It's now filled with families holding bags containing any one of the dozens of "Alcatraz Athletic Dept." T-shirts, colorful sunglasses, imitation prison garb, magnets, or coffee mugs. Perhaps it helps to make light of it; the reality can be dark. To enter these tiny, decrepit cells, to stand behind these metal bars, and to imagine them filled with men is a heavy thought. It's easier to pose behind the bars, to laugh, to buy a T-shirt, and to go home.

Yet there are still poignant elements to make you think about day-to-day prison life, for both prisoners and staff. The large showers used to screen incoming inmates; the kitchen area that features an outline of each knife painted on the wall, so that the kitchen crew knew where to return it, and so that it would be easier to tell if one went missing. Above the counter in front is a black felt board with tiny white plastic letters spelling out the menu items for breakfast in the kitchen area. The sign read: "21 Marc 963"; presumably the "h" and the "1" are missing. Below that it says: Assorted dry cereals, steamed wheat, 1 scrambled egg, 2 milk, stewed fruit, toast, bread, butter, coffee.

I took a photo and texted it along with the message "They got hot breakfast!" to my mom, whom we tease about the simple breakfasts she served us during our high school years. My mom would hand us chocolate-chip granola bars at 7 a.m. as we rushed out to the minivan in which she drove us to school. "OK, let's say our Hail Marys," she'd call, and we'd pray ten Hail Marys together with mouths full of granola. "You probably had better roommates," she wrote back.

On my way out, I passed through another gift shop, with magnets on which were written various Alcatraz regulations. One read: "Alcatraz Regulation #5: You are entitled to food, clothing, shelter, and medical attention. Anything else you get is a privilege." I couldn't help but think that, with the addition of a few basic freedoms, this applied outside the walls of the prison as well.

Now as I enter San Quentin, I'm surprised to find yet another gift shop. It's a small room attached to the guard station and the bathroom just outside the prison gates. I wander inside with some caution. The low, glass-front display cases are filled with various handcrafted items: drawings and paintings, a variety of leather goods—including a wallet with the name Loraine burned into it, a bracelet that reads Norma, and another saying San Quentin. The market for these items seems limited, and something about them seems especially poignant to me. I can't help but wonder if they were made with someone in mind, a person the crafter hopes will visit someday. A guy drops off a leather belt for some repair work. I walk around slowly and notice a red-orange leather bracelet with a gold snap fastener. The man behind the counter puts it on the counter and I try it on. It fits, and I pay a few dollars for it. It costs less than my poncho did the day before.

I realize it's time to meet up with Fr. George Williams, a Jesuit priest and the prison chaplain at San Quentin, so I head back to the car to drop off my belongings. I have been communicating with Fr. Williams by e-mail for weeks in preparation for this visit. Just two days ago we officially confirmed when and where I'd meet him (by the front gate, 8:30 a.m.). He added a few tips to the end of his e-mail:

> Don't wear blue clothes. No open-toe shoes. Bring your driver's license. Leave all drugs, knives, guns, and cell phones in car.
> Thanks,
> Fr. Williams

His tips gave me pause. While leaving behind guns, drugs, and knives was hardly a sacrifice, I sit for a moment in my car wearing a red, long-sleeved blouse, black trousers, and loafers, holding an internal debate about whether or not my denim jacket qualified as blue. I determine that it isn't worth risking, whatever the reason I wasn't supposed to wear it, and I leave it in the car before entering the chilly San Francisco air on my way to the gate and whatever lay beyond it.

CHAPTER 20

—IN WHICH I TALK ABOUT DEATH ROW AND ST. DISMAS WITH A PRISON CHAPLAIN

The death row inmates at San Quentin State Prison live in East Block, a long, tall structure with a red-brown roof and imposing concrete sides. Thin barred windows run down the dirty exterior walls, but none lets in much light. Cells measuring four feet by ten feet are stacked five levels high, and the whole place feels like a kind of kennel. In what might be called a foyer, if the structure were a suburban home, barbed wire rises up and around a gate separating the inmates from the entryway and the door, which is large and metal and has painted above it on the outside the word *Condemned* in black calligraphy. This door leads back to the prison yard, through which it is possible to walk toward a seemingly countless number of other gates and doors, some of which eventually lead to the outside world, or "the street," as some of the men call it.

Five days a week, Fr. Williams steps into San Quentin from the outside to fulfill his role as chaplain. Twice a week, he walks through the doors and gates and past the barbed wire, through the darkness of East Block, to the cells where more than seven hundred men live alone, together. There he puts on a black bulletproof vest—a requirement for all who enter the cell block—that matches his clerical garb. He then spends hours listening to any inmate who needs to be heard. "A lot of them just long to talk to a human being who will listen and respond with respect and interest," he says, as he guides me through the maze of the prison. "I've gotten feedback from people who say, 'You're the only person who bothers to talk to me.'"

The first time he entered East Block, Fr. Williams was surprised by the heaviness of the place, its depth, its "atmosphere of oppression." But gradually he began to notice the light. "There's darkness in there that's real and palpable," he says later, as we sit on two metal folding chairs in the small classroom next to the chapel. "But there's also goodness in there. Even in the guys who have done horrible things, I see the goodness in them."

On my way in I pass through the office of a correctional officer. The officer checks me in and searches the bag in which I carry my recording equipment. He pulls out the recording equipment and questions me. As he does so, he makes an inventory on a piece of paper from a greying legal pad. I tell him there are earbuds in the front pouch. He zips open the pocket to check. "Nothing is a given here," he says, somewhat forebodingly.

A small group of students (who also happen to be inmates, not on death row) are expected to arrive soon. I'm planning to interview them about the theology classes Fr. Williams teaches. The classroom to which Fr. Williams has led me is small and lined with shelves filled with colorful books. A beige statue of the Virgin and Child sits in a niche, below a panoramic photograph of Nazareth and beside a painting of the Last Supper. On a stack of metal folding chairs the words "Catholic Chapel" are stenciled in black paint. From inside the room, a visitor could easily mistake it for any other religious education classroom. It is only when one steps outside that the guards and the gates and the barbed wire that make up so much of San Quentin State

Prison become visible. It is then that you remember this is no ordinary classroom.

Fr. Williams tells me that for a while he made a point of reading about the crimes each man had committed. Eventually, he stopped. He told himself, *I don't need to know this.* "It's horror movie stuff, some of it," he says. "The men are on death row because they did horrible crimes. But they're not horrible human beings. There are other dimensions to them besides that. They're not murderers. They've *committed* murder, maybe several. But they are *still* human beings who did these things. They are not the crime."

I consider the number of people who have slighted me over the years. I consider the ways in which I have sometimes defined these people by these slights; the way I've sometimes held on to these far smaller offenses. Forgiveness is always a challenge.

Fr. Williams recalls one day when he was leaving the cell of a man convicted of committing serial murders. The inmate waved good-bye, saying, "See you later. Don't do anything I wouldn't do." Fr. Williams couldn't help but laugh. "There are moments like that," he says. "It's dark humor but it's funny. For the prisoners themselves, there's little to laugh about being in prison. It's a horrible thing to go through. But I think the ones who keep their focus on the world and don't turn inward and let the place get to them, they do better. Laughing about it helps."

Perhaps I had been too quick to judge some of the levity surrounding my trip to Alcatraz; perhaps some of the men whose voices I heard would have been the first to laugh at the antics I saw. Fr. Williams has tried to add a little more light to the prison through the theology classes he teaches.

Fr. Williams recruited a few volunteer teachers to teach a total of four classes: Introduction to Church Teaching, Introduction to Jesuit Spirituality, Church History, and Philosophy as an Introduction to

Theology. Each class is different, and each teacher is free to take his or her own approach. Fr. Williams uses DVDs, along with portions of the *Catechism* to teach his class. He often pauses the videos to discuss the topics with the men. He stresses to the men that he is not there just to teach doctrine, but to think and to approach the church with questions. He says they want to know what the church thinks about the death penalty. They're interested in how the church explains the nature of God and Jesus and the Trinity. "I tell these guys, 'Don't just take in what I say or what the *Catechism* says. Think about it. Use your brain. Because God gave us brains and hearts, and he expects us to use both.'" He continues, "I have a sense that they are searching and trying to make meaning out of the experiences of their own lives. Trying to make sense of the question: If there's a loving God, then how come there are places like this?"

Three of the classes meet in the small classroom we're sitting in, and one meets in the large chapel nearby. Fr. Williams sees the classes as personal enrichment and a chance to deepen their spiritual lives. He hopes the Jesuit spirituality class may one day lend itself to holding retreats, of a sort, for the men. San Quentin is unusually open to creating new rehabilitative programs for inmates, and those in charge of the prison were receptive to and grateful for Fr. Williams's idea. The inmates were as well.

"Was it always like that?" I wonder.

"No, it's gone through stages," he says. "The 1970s were very violent. And we all went through this lockdown stage in the 1980s and 1990s as rehabilitation went out the window. But there's an interest in social justice here, and the local community has always kept an eye on San Quentin and stayed involved in the process here and contributed a lot to make sure the prisoners got good programming."

"I think there is something about being in this environment that brings the Scriptures alive in a way you don't get in a parish," he says.

"Over at death row we're talking now about the passion of Christ. He was sentenced to death; they're sentenced to death. There are so many parallels. Being arrested, put on trial—unfairly, in Jesus' case—and then sentenced to be executed, and being executed by the state. It's uncanny how you read these stories in a different light here."

Fr. Williams shows me a painting completed in 1986 by Fernando Caro, an inmate on death row. The image is one of St. Dismas, the apocryphal name given to the "good thief," the one who asked Jesus to remember him after death. (Not to be confused with the other one, the one my sister played in the Passion play, sometimes known as Gestas). I am struck by the artist's desire, which I share, to find saints and figures in Scripture with whom to relate. St. Dismas wouldn't have been my first choice, but I can see the appeal for Fernando, and I can see the care he has taken in depicting this figure. The image is one of a man with a tanned face and trimmed beard. He wears a short white tunic with sandals and a fuzzy light brown cloak. He holds a staff in one hand and has a long sword attached to his belt. The figure stands against a blue background and by his feet, in the bottom corners of the paintings, are two tiny scenes in black and white. The bottom right has a depiction of Golgotha, with three men hanging, crucified. The bottom left has the Holy Family on their way to Egypt, a tiny St. Dismas standing beside them.

I wonder aloud what that represents. Fr. Williams tells me that, apparently, the same tradition that has given the two criminals names, "The Arabic Gospel of the Infancy," also presents another apocryphal story. In this version, Dismas and Gestas attempt to rob the Holy Family on their journey to Egypt, but Dismas decides against it and convinces Gestas otherwise. At this point, the always-prescient baby Jesus predicts that they would meet again in Jerusalem, where they would be crucified together, and that Dismas would join him in paradise.

It's a fascinating bit of lore, and I can see why it would appeal to those in prison. And why art—the bracelets and paintings—would appeal to them as well. Fr. Williams comments, "A lot of these guys who have come from addictive pasts tend to want something they can see and touch when talking about spiritual things. And I think that's where we have a real gift in the Catholic Church; we use all our senses in prayer."

Many of the men at San Quentin are serving sentences ranging from fifteen years to life in prison. Many already have done twenty or thirty years. It's not a "starter" prison. Many are serving time for violent crimes but have been moved to San Quentin for good behavior.

Most of the men understand that they have a real opportunity for growth here. So the classes sell themselves. The men who attend them want to be there. "Prisoners are some of the best students because they really want to learn," Fr. Williams says. "A lot of them, for whatever reason, were not given the opportunity. They were told they were stupid, or they didn't have good schools, or there was so much dysfunction they didn't go to school. . . . I've found it really difficult over the past seventeen years to find a way to get people on the outside to think about people in prison outside of a stereotype, to see them as human beings capable of change, and also to recognize our responsibility as Christians to be with them in that change both while they're in prison and while they're out."

"If there's one thing in prison that people desire, it's forgiveness," Fr. Williams says to me. "And often self-forgiveness is the hardest part. . . . Confession is profoundly healing for the guys in here, and it's my favorite part of being here, really. In prison, that's where the rubber meets the road—in the reconciliation room."

Even within the prison there are additional limits. Around certain areas there are lines painted on the ground. If inmates cross them, it is considered an escape attempt. So it's no wonder that they seek some sort of freedom through spiritual growth. And in a strange way, I can understand. I often find that it's the times when I feel the least in control, when I am the most confused, that I reach out to God in prayer most completely. It's these times when I'm able to truly give myself over to God's will.

For the condemned prisoners on death row, an old shower room covered with a large cage serves as a chapel. Fr. Williams stands on one side of the heavy metal grill, like that of a cloistered monastery. The prisoners stand on the other side, three of whom require their own cages. He hands out the Eucharist through a sort of mail slot in the grate. They have slots in each cage, he tells me, and when they do the sign of peace, they can reach out to each other. One time an inmate held up his fingertip to a tiny hole in the grate. Fr. Williams placed his hand against the grate as well.

"It really sums up the whole thing. You have this human being reaching through a cage to touch another human being within a bigger cage, within a prison."

CHAPTER 21

—IN WHICH I DISCUSS FAITH AND MIDWESTERN FRIENDLINESS WITH SEVERAL INMATES

Johnny is the first inmate to arrive, and I'm surprised by how sweet he looks. He has shaggy brown curls and a soft face. He appears to be the sort of guy you wouldn't hesitate to ask directions from on the street. He's wearing a chain with a large crucifix and a medal of the Virgin Mary, which he bought before he even became Catholic. He's wearing dark blue cotton pants that say "Prisoner" in bright yellow letters down the front of the right leg, and a light blue top with a bright yellow jacket over it. Now I understand the ban on blue clothes. Before I arrived, I struggled with whether or not I should ask the men about their crimes, or even to find out ahead of time, with a quick Internet search or e-mail to Fr. Williams, what they were. I decide not to do either, so I am working only from first impressions.

I introduce myself, and Johnny shakes my hand. He seems shy and is soft-spoken and seemingly unsure of what he's about to do. Then we begin to discuss his faith. Johnny tells me he was baptized in 2010, and since then he's tried hard to learn as much as possible about the Catholic Church. He works as an assistant clerk in the chapel, in order to stay as close as possible—physically, spiritually—to the church. He helps fill requests from prisoners who can't get to the chapel, sending them Bibles, prayer cards, or rosaries.

He grew up in a nondenominational household and never went to church. After entering San Quentin, he began exploring the various chaplaincies. "It was always the Catholic Church where I felt most comfortable," he says. "Maybe that's because of the family setting here, with the Father and with Virgin Mary as our mother and all the angels and saints. It felt more like a family here than anywhere else."

In the six weeks since he's been taking the church history class, he's learned about topics from the Gospels to Roman emperors. He's learning about the Spiritual Exercises of St. Ignatius, which he has discovered he can relate to. "Some of the practices I'm learning are things I'd done on my own before I even was aware of the class or St. Ignatius. You can just place yourself into the prayers you're doing or the meditations you're doing. With the spirituality practices you can sort of put yourself there with Christ as he's going through whatever he's going through."

What he describes isn't all that far off from what I experienced at Xavier a few days earlier at the stations of the cross. The universal nature of prayer never ceases to amaze me.

Taking the classes has encouraged Johnny not just personally but also in the way he interacts with others around him. "In here there are so many people who seem to be discouraged or upset or angry, and what we're learning from the church are ways that we can reach out to them, without so much trying to convert them to anything," says Johnny. "Whether that's giving them a sandwich or just talking to them in general to make them feel better; to let them know that, even if they don't have anybody on the street, there's someone here they can talk to. Instead of recognizing them as another prisoner and just walking past them like robots, you can take the time to see if there's something wrong with them and actually help them."

I think of the people I've passed by. I think of the ways in which I've acted like a robot.

The more Johnny learns, the more he wants to share. He says he's grateful to be at San Quentin because of the classes. He's only thirty-five, but he's spent sixteen years incarcerated. The three months he's spent at San Quentin have been among the best; he's also been involved with a restorative justice program and self-help classes, as well as environmental awareness and preservation groups. "The more I learn, and the more I want to share with others, and the more I meditate on things I'm doing in the church program, the better I am at learning more about who I used to be and how I'm different now, and what motivated me to do what I did to get to be here. And in that way not only am I helping myself, but I can help other people who are just learning more about the programs. Before I always thought about what was best for me, and I never thought about what was best for anyone else. But what I'm learning in the church, at least for me, is that you try to do for others first. That way you're always taken care of, because while you're busy doing for others, God is taking care of you." I can't help but think of the good thief. I say a prayer to St. Dismas, who may be apocryphal but at this moment feels very real.

Next to arrive is Kevin, thirty-seven, who was raised Catholic and has spent the past twenty-two years in prison. Fifty-year-old Alan joins us as well; he was baptized last year at San Quentin. Kevin sports a denim jacket with an American flag pin on the lapel. We talk about struggling with anger. About struggling with forgiveness. About playing the guitar at Mass. They are topics not far removed from my own life.

Each man agreed that the overall atmosphere of San Quentin is positive, one that encourages good behavior and community. Both are taking the theology classes. "It's teaching me a lot about forgiveness.

About forgiving myself for what's happened with addiction and the causes that make us what we are today," Alan said. "And it's a struggle."

Kevin, who has been in San Quentin since December 2011, says, "We're human beings, and most of us come here with a sincere heart, despite any of the things we may have done in the past. And some things are violent and terrible. But not everybody is just an animal who is locked up. We are human beings; we have feelings and emotions like everybody else, and to be judged by just a small portion of our lives compared to the totality of our lives is wrong."

Kevin continues: "This class isn't just something people come to, to hide behind the Bible or to try and find a way to get the parole board to let them out. Some of us have no chance of getting out, and yet we still continue to come here because we find the enrichment very fulfilling." Kevin adds how much Fr. Williams has been a blessing to them there. "He doesn't lump us all together. We're each individuals, and that's a positive thing."

Finally, Ed joins us. He was raised in Oakland, California, and has been incarcerated for thirteen years and in San Quentin for two and a half. He's fifty-nine and the gruffest of the group. For him the classes represent a kind of freedom. "For me it's extremely important because I only have two things in this environment and one is my spirituality and my ability to come and participate in religious services. And the other is my communication with my daughters. That is about all I have. And the likelihood of my getting out is very, very remote at best." In his spiritual life, he has found comfort in the life of St. Paul. "He has been one that's 'been there, done that.'"

I am so engrossed in our conversation that I forget for a moment that they are prisoners. Later, when I go home, I will search for their names online, and their crimes will make me shudder. But in that moment, Fr. Williams has stepped away, and I am just standing in the lobby of the chapel waiting for him to return, talking to these men about the differences between the East Coast and the Midwest and whose residents seem friendlier. And they are speaking with respect and laughter. I had arrived ready to visit prisoners, but if I'm honest, I did not arrive ready to visit people.

Finally, Fr. Williams walks me back out of the facility, and we squint as we walk into the sunny parking lot. We pass huge groups of prisoners in blue and denim. So much of prison life is about labels and boundaries. Some prisoners wear blue, along with jackets like the denim one I (fortunately) left behind. Others are in orange or white. Apparently the men in white have the most potential for danger.

"It's very surreal," I say. "It doesn't seem like the people I spoke with are capable of doing the things that got them here."

Fr. Williams looks up. "We're all capable of doing what put them here," he says. "Some of these guys come from foster care or their mothers were prostitutes." I think about circumstances. None of these things means that these men were destined to become criminals, but it certainly didn't make their lives any easier. And I realize that in some ways there's very little separating those of us who buy novelty T-shirts at the Alcatraz gift shop from those who make leather goods for the shop at San Quentin: a different family, a few wrong choices. It's hard to say what motivates people to do the things they do. Like the correctional officer said, nothing is a given.

CHAPTER 22

—IN WHICH I LEARN NOT TO MAKE ASSUMPTIONS ABOUT WHO IS SICK

My friend Sister Camille, who is almost eighty, agrees to drive me to visit the sick, although technically most of the women we're going to see have spent more time visiting the sick themselves than being visited. We're headed to the Holy Thursday liturgy at the home for retired Sisters of Mercy. It's a sunny day, and one of the first things I see upon entering the home is a large tapestry that looks like a stained-glass window in which the Corporal Works of Mercy are written. We're greeted by a spry Sr. Aileen, who is recovering from surgery but otherwise looks quite well. She ushers us into a community room, where we sit at a long, rectangular table. Moments later we're joined by five other sisters. Most look quite well, especially considering they are in their seventies or eighties.

Sr. Camille kicks off our conversation with memories of Sr. Marie, who did a lot of visiting of the sick and then suffered a spinal injury that left her paralyzed from the waist down. "I remember her saying, 'Visit the sick, and don't stay too long, and then leave, unless they ask you to stay.'" The sisters nod in agreement.

Sr. Kathleen says she has both visited the sick and been visited, and she's found receiving the visits more difficult than doing the visiting. "Our life was a life of doing—and when you're sick, it impedes your obligation. But it was one of the most effective times in my life because I had to depend solely on the Lord," she said. "It's difficult to have someone do for you all the things you used to do for yourself." Right now she is recuperating from knee replacement and two major back surgeries. The sisters talk about the way they care for one another, and how they try to anticipate each person's needs and do for her what she can't do for herself, and how they are energized by the stories they tell one another.

Sr. Kathleen has spent time volunteering as a hospital chaplain: "We visit everyone," she says, adding that generally people are grateful to see you. The patients worry about their families, too. "It's invigorating to see how people cope," she says. "They light up when you come into the room, but it's more about their faith in God and trust." She visits a woman with Lou Gehrig's disease who used to be a head nurse at a hospital. Now she can't speak or move, and she worries about who will care for her husband, who has Alzheimer's. This faith is so tangible that Sr. Kathleen feels like taking off her shoes upon entering this woman's room. "You see the things that people worry about, but you also become aware of the goodness of other people," she says.

I saw this firsthand when I had an emergency appendectomy a few years back. I tend to imagine I have every possible illness, but when my stomachache wouldn't go away, I knew I had to go to the hospital. I did not want to admit that I needed some help, but my then-boyfriend (God bless him, the same man who'd been punched in the face by the homeless man) came out to Queens from the Bronx to ride in the cab with me to the hospital, because I could barely stand up; he sat beside me when I began vomiting into a paper bag in the waiting room, as everyone else moved further away; he comforted me as I sat waiting for test results on a gurney in a hallway.

Hours later, my bed had been moved to the foot of the nurses' desk, which was mostly out of the way, although it placed me precariously close to the gangrenous foot of a man being wheeled away on another gurney. When my boyfriend had to leave for work, my roommate showed up and sat with me as I waited in a bay. She laughed with me when I told her that the man who brought me to get various tests was named (I swear) Devil (it was on his name tag). I was there only a few days, but people came to see me anyway. They sent flowers; they made calls. My friend Tim brought me a badge that said "Winner" to wear on my hospital gown, because that's the sort of thing we do. And when the time came to leave, another friend came and guided me home in a cab, carrying my belongings because I couldn't lift them. I had never felt weaker or more loved. And maybe that's part of what visiting the sick is about—being open and loving to people who are more vulnerable than they'd like to be.

Sr. Camille has read quite a bit on the history of the community and adds to the conversation that the sick aren't the only people the sisters have a habit of visiting. In the 1890s the Sisters of Mercy went regularly to visit the Raymond Street jail in Brooklyn. They made the trip on foot. Many of the prisoners were Irish, poor, out of work, and uneducated. The sisters would write letters for them and teach them about religion. One day they approached a man who had a death sentence. He rebuked them and said he was innocent. Weeks went by, and he watched the sisters interact with the other men. Finally, he said he wanted to see them. They went to him, and he eventually became Catholic, and in the end he also became the last man to die by hanging in New York State. And after his execution, the person who committed the crime confessed to it. "Visiting prisons was always an early work," Sr. Camille says, admitting that this seems off-topic, but adding, "There's more than a physical sickness involved in this. There's the excruciating sickness of loneliness and alienation and condemnation."

I think about the men I met at San Quentin—their loneliness, their desire to belong. I look around the table at the women and realize that no matter what they're recovering from, they make an effort to be there to support one another, so that none is sick of heart. Maybe, I think, the point is not to seek out the sick. Maybe it's just to recognize when people are not well, whether it's because they're physically ill or lonely, whether that means Adam staying up all night with his ailing grandmother or sitting down to talk with someone. Maybe there's far less bureaucracy involved in this than I thought.

"What are ways to help cope with sickness of your own?" I ask the sisters.

"We have the Blessed Sacrament and prayer," says one sister. "What you can't understand, God understands. I just try to be where the sisters are. You don't think 'poor me.' The fact that we are so close helps in any recovery, more than any pill."

Sr. Kathleen speaks up again: "I try to put myself in the hands of God. I love the freedom that age brings. We're free here. I'm free because I do place myself in God's presence and I give myself over. I don't have to worry about what's coming tomorrow. I don't have to worry about money. I would love to be active in ministry, but I can be active here. Living the now. That's the answer for me anyway."

And among the seven sisters around me there are 452 years of service to the church. They have served in inner-city parishes, in schools, in hospitals; and now here, they serve one another. It's a fitting image for Holy Thursday. Later, at Mass, as the priest kneels to wash a few sisters' feet, I can't help but think of the many ways in which they've done the same to all those they have served through the years. It also reminds me of a moment I experienced during my year as a volunteer special education teacher in the Navajo Nation in Arizona.

One afternoon, one of the students in my class wasn't feeling well. She was nonverbal, so she couldn't really tell us how she was feeling, and sometimes she forgot to tell us that she needed to use the toilet. On this day she was too ill to tell us anything at all, and she got sick all over herself. All over. I took her to help her get cleaned up, and I was feeling both a bit grossed out and a bit self-congratulatory for taking this on. She was quite small, so when I knelt down, I was at about eye level with her.

She put her hand on my shoulder to steady herself and just looked at me expectantly, knowing that I would help her and with this look that sort of said, *OK, go ahead, and do what you're supposed to do.* And I knew right away that what I was doing did not make me special. It was just exactly the sort of attention and care for others that I needed to be showing, in some form, every day. I have never felt so clearly that I was looking into the face of Christ as when I saw her looking at me that day. That's how I picture God, someone who says, *OK, let's go. Do what you've been called to do.* And that is what we're all called to do: to love and serve.

CHAPTER 23

—IN WHICH I CARRY A CROSS AND GO ON THE WORLD'S MOST PIOUS DATE

My second attempt at praying the stations of the cross begins in Dag Hammarskjöld plaza, near the United Nations. The morning is cheerful and sunny, if somewhat cool. I'm heading to the stations of the cross sponsored by Pax Christi, a Catholic organization of peace activists. The stations are a longtime tradition in the city, and the event offers a new way for me to pray this old devotion. It also means that I'll follow through on my promise to pray the stations twice this Lent. I am somewhat uneasy about being part of such a public and vocal display of religion, particularly one in which I will be marching through the street, singing in Latin, and following a flatbed truck carrying a guitarist, a flutist, and four large speakers. It's not that I'm ashamed of my faith; it's just that I've always been more drawn to the St. Francis philosophy: "Preach the gospel at all times; if necessary, use words." He said nothing about sound systems.

Upon my arrival, I immediately run into friends and acquaintances from other New York City Catholic ministries. There's still a part of me that's surprised to run into people I know in New York, which even after almost five years feels new in so many ways. But seeing familiar faces gives the city a small-town feel; it makes me feel a bit more at home.

One of these people is Lynn, a woman I know from a volunteer group; I wave. I'm happy to see her, and she greets me excitedly, as well. "Kerry, we need someone to carry the cross," she says. I freeze. I was not planning on this. She senses my discomfort. "It's just one station," she says.

"Do I have to carry it over my shoulder?" I ask, not confident in my abilities. She says no, just carry it in front of you, held high. I very much want to say no. And yet, I hear myself saying yes. "Great," she says, adding that I should join the front of the group before the eighth station begins. I fall into the crowd, which snakes slowly through the streets following the truck and the singers, while singing meditation chants. Reflections are shared at each station, and I stand with my mouth agape as one woman describes being tricked into moving to the United States only to have her kidney removed for illegal organ sales while she was trapped in a basement. I am struck by the level of suffering that goes on around me, here in New York, in the country, in the world, that I will never know about.

We continue walking down 42nd Street, and as we arrive near Bryant Park I move toward the front of the line and take up my cross. As the folks on the truck begin to drive away and the crowd behind me starts singing, I pick it up and begin walking slowly toward Times Square. The last time I walked down this block, I was on a date. Now as I move forward, a sort of Jesus in skinny jeans and a plaid scarf, I am no longer self-conscious about holding the cross. I feel more relaxed, I feel supported by the song of the people behind me. Along the way, people stare at us and snap pictures and gawk. Or, because it is New York, many just pass us by with a slight sigh, their eyes on the ground.

As we reach Times Square, the truck stops near the armed forces recruiting center there. Sr. Camille has climbed up on the flatbed giving a reflection on the death penalty and forgiveness; behind her are huge lights set up for a Pepsi photo shoot. We are surrounded by billboards for clothing lines and fast food. And somehow it all seems perfect, this strange nexus of the sacred and secular, the prayers and songs seeming to bless the entire neighborhood.

The juxtaposition of unlikely events is at the core of Good Friday: a death that brings life. It is saying yes to whatever cross Christ asks you to bear, even if it's awkward or heavy and it means you may suffer or that strangers will take photos of you with their cell phones as you lead several hundred Catholics to Times Square.

It would be foolish to say that New York has saved me, but it would be lying to say that it hasn't shaped me. I sometimes feel the same way about the church as I do about the city itself: it can seem illogical and overwhelming, but it can also be powerful, creative, and diverse. People are constantly asking me about it: "Why do you stay?" "Aren't the people there unwelcoming and curmudgeonly?" And I sometimes can't believe that I'm lumped in with certain crowds, forced into close quarters with people I might otherwise avoid.

"What about the cost?" people wonder. "There are so many things you have to give up." And sometimes I think they're right; sometimes I feel like it's not worth it. But most of the time I look around and it seems like a miracle that this community has continued through so much, over so many years, filled with so many changes. And I see so many people trying to do good; so many people trying to better themselves. And most of the time I'm glad to be a part of it all.

I appreciate that both the church and my city are greater than the sum of their flaws, that at their best they are both places that inspire good. They are fluid, with people coming and going all the time—looking for new starts, hiding from old hurts, finding comfort. People think, *I'm going to be a new person here.*

When the procession is over, I grab a quick cup of tea, to stave off my increasing hunger from the traditional Good Friday fasting (which works just like Ash Wednesday: very small meals). I haven't eaten all day, but it occurs to me that I haven't really been hungry. There was so much else to feel, to consider, to contemplate. So much that I had opened myself up to because I wasn't looking at menus in the windows of the restaurants we passed or worrying about spending too much on an overpriced sandwich. Instead of feeling grumpy from hunger, I felt free.

I throw away my empty cup and head over to the Good Friday liturgy at St. Paul the Apostle, where I will venerate the cross, a tradition in which the congregation slowly processes forward and one by one kisses a huge statue of the crucified Christ. In terms of Lenten practices, this one ranks right up there with the stations of the cross in terms of my enthusiasm.

I have told Adam that I can meet up with him afterward. We have decided that if we share a bowl of soup and some bread we'll be in keeping with the rules of the fast and also feel less guilty about maybe going to a movie afterward. So I'm surprised when he texts me to say that he's decided to come to the liturgy, as well. The church is packed and because we have to go up twice, once for veneration of the cross and again for communion, the lines are seemingly endless, and I have lots of time to contemplate Christ's sacrifice, and whether or not Adam is having a good time. Yet the inviting, diverse congregation, the energetic homily, and the lovely music make the time pass fairly quickly. Every once in a while I glance over at Adam, who as far as I can tell does not seem completely miserable. I'm looking forward to the soup. As we near the end of the liturgy, he looks up and grins and whispers: "I get to pick the third date."

CHAPTER 24

—IN WHICH I GO TO A CEMETERY TO REMEMBER THAT I'M ALIVE

I do not have extensive experience with either the beginning or the end stages of life. The closest I have come to birth is that I once, while staying at a Massachusetts farm, helped a sheep that was giving birth to a lamb, whose leg was caught in the birth canal. I reached inside the sheep and pulled out the lamb, and it was one of the most beautiful, and slimy, experiences I've had.

As a member of an Irish-Catholic family and a granddaughter of a couple who had many friends who became like family, during my childhood I spent a fair amount of time attending wakes. But the person whose death I recall most clearly from those years is my grandfather. Perhaps because I was there not just for the funeral and wake, but for much of his long, slow decline as the skin cancer ate away at him.

My siblings and I would accompany Mom to my grandfather's house. He wore a large bandage across much of his face, and my mom often cleaned the wound and spent time with my grandfather. The house, which years earlier often smelled of hot dogs or microwave popcorn or lamb stew or pot roast, when my grandmother was alive to cook these things, now seemed not only to feel heavier but also to smell horribly, of illness combined with a scented candle meant to cover it up.

Sometimes my cousins would be there too, and they'd join me and my brother as we ran upstairs to the attic, which always seemed far removed from whatever went on below. The attic was filled with unused china and an old-fashioned pram, vases and old telephones, bowls and shelves and desks, all things that seemed like treasures, a fact confirmed by an old cardboard sign with painted red letters that read "Attic Treasures." The attic also contained a kind of barrel, a cylindrical cardboard tube into which we'd take turns crawling and then bracing ourselves against the side while pushing each other across the floor, growing dizzier and dizzier until for a moment we'd forget how close we were to the heaviness of the house below.

When my grandfather died, I remember crying. I remember missing him. I remember climbing into a limo outside our church on the way to the cemetery and feeling like the limo was kind of cool, and wondering if thinking that might be a sin. I remember looking down into the grave and seeing concrete and being surprised and thinking it strange that eternal life should be so confining.

So I was interested in learning more about burying the dead in New York. But unfortunately, it's not exactly an easy task to accomplish in New York. My e-mail asking to interview inmates who dug graves on Hart Island received a less than encouraging reply in which the communications officer wrote, in part:

> Thanks for your interest in the NYC Department of Correction. Unfortunately, we will not be able to accommodate your request for a visit to Hart Island due to safety and security concerns. As you may know, inmates bury the dead on the Island under the supervision of Correction personnel, therefore the interview you are requesting is completely inappropriate—again, for safety and security concerns.

He then offered to answer specific questions and directed me to an unofficial history site. I'd also written to and called the Old Calvary Cemetery, which is the largest in the country, to see if I could go out with a gravedigger or even just chat with one, but I'd never heard from them.

So, denied that way of proceeding, the best I could think of was simply to visit the old cemetery. I wasn't sure, but it seemed the closest I was going to get to burying the dead was to spend some time around the dead who were already buried.

I decide to jog to the cemetery, and possibly through it, on Saturday morning. The cemetery is less than a mile from my apartment, but I have never really been inside the walls. I expect a kind of somber dreariness to the place, but pink budding trees are before me, and two rabbits are hopping across a fresh, green lawn. It's gorgeous, and I'm stopped in my tracks, stunned by the juxtaposition of so much life and death all in the same place.

I wander among the grave stones, many large and elaborate, some old, with worn out angels' faces; others new with laser-cut portraits of loved ones' faces.

Then I see an older man waiting near an official-looking truck and wearing khaki and green. I walk up to him and ask what he does at the cemetery, although I am fairly certain I know the answer. He smiles and confirms my suspicion that he is, in fact, a gravedigger. He tells me his name is Stanley, and that he is sixty-three and from Poland.

"Does your job make you think about death a lot?" I ask, cutting to the chase.

"No, everybody have to die," he says through a thick accent. "You don't know when. You are young so you don't have to think like me. Sixty-three years old is different."

"Well, you never know," I say.

"I know." He says, "I know."

"Do you feel a connection to the people whose graves you're digging?"

"No. I never think of this because you work so many years. You have your job. You work your job; I work my job. Same thing. You secretary, you work as secretary. In my job, digging graves and fill in graves. I just do my job. You have to be careful because when digging grave maybe one body is already buried. You can't touch other caskets."

"What do you use, a backhoe?"

"A big backhoe."

"Are you looking forward to retirement, or will you miss this?"

"Ah, time come you have to go," he says. "I think I go sixty-five."

"This seems like a good place to be," I add.

"It's not bad," he says. "But you have to like this job. Some people cut grass. They like cut grass. Some people don't like cut grass. You know."

"The grave digging is your thing, huh?"

"The grave digging is different. You dig and then you have to relax; wait for the burial. Come in. People go away. You go to fill in."

Stanley seems like he's itching to get back to his truck, so I let him go and thank him and keep walking. I wanted him to say something profound, something that conveys the spiritual significance of what he does.

I sit on a stone step and give Adam a call. He's out to brunch with his mother after having spent the night caring for his grandmother, who couldn't sleep and was growing increasingly confused. He asks me how my Works of Mercy are going, and as I start to tell him, I realize that perhaps I haven't been paying enough attention to the ones he is doing. As I scrambled around the city looking for people to care for, he had been doing so quietly at home, taking care of his grandmother, trying to give his mother a break. And preparing for the very real possibility of burying the dead. Teddy Roosevelt is credited with saying, "Do what you can, with what you have, where you are." That seemed to be Adam's approach to these Works of Mercy, and it was a powerful one. I wasn't sure whether or not my relationship with Adam would last (spoiler alert: it didn't), but I knew that this lesson would.

As I hang up the phone and start walking, there's a grandeur to the whole cemetery that seems bittersweet. I wonder how many of these people have relatives living today. How many are thought of by people other than those who cut the grass or drive by? And so I take a moment to think of them, to consider the fact that each of the stone markers before me represents a once living, breathing person: native New Yorkers, immigrants, old, tragically young. Everyone with a story to tell, a story I would never know, and yet know intimately because it is the story we all tell. Maybe my typical day and Stanley's weren't so different after all: You dig in; people come and go. You try to relax and enjoy the beauty around you. And in the end you just hope you've done what was asked of you and filled it all up as best you can. As I walk, I put in my earbuds and turn on Bruce Springsteen's latest album and pull up the song "We Are Alive." And the words sound less like rock'n'roll and more like a hymn. And the graves seem to be shouting to me: "We are not here. Let the dead bury the dead!" And suddenly I am running again, and the pink blossoms fall from the trees around me as I take my first steps toward home.

CHAPTER 25

—IN WHICH I GET LOCKED OUT OF THE CHURCH WHILE TRYING TO HELP PEOPLE ENTER IT

I can't help smiling as I walk up 5th Avenue toward St. Patrick's Cathedral's gift shop on a windy Saturday in the late afternoon. In a few short hours, Lauren, Zubair, Jackie, and about a dozen others will become full members of the Catholic Church. I'm thrilled that I will soon share my favorite night in the church with these individuals. I'm honored to have shared in a special part of their spiritual journey. Also, I'm really looking forward to the cake. After forty-some days without sweets, I can't wait to partake in cupcakes in the back of the church after Mass. And then, possibly later in the evening, the Cherry Garcia ice cream I've already stashed in the freezer. These last few hours of Lent are sort of beautifully strange, when I feel both a kind of accomplishment and a relief. There has been so much to process over the past several weeks, and I'm still discovering what it will mean going forward.

But, first, I must focus on tonight. I have decided to buy a St. Thérèse of Lisieux medal for Lauren as a confirmation gift, in honor of her confirmation name, which is a name each candidate and catechumen symbolically takes on to represent this new stage of his or her spiritual life. The gift shop is surprisingly busy, but not too crowded, and I quickly purchase the medal and stow it in my purse before walking over to St. Paul the Apostle Church. I am planning to meet Lauren at Starbucks ahead of time, and she arrives with Zubair. They both look excited. We decide to take a walk around the block to kill some time.

It is surprisingly chilly as we walk slowly around the block. Zubair laughs. "If you had told me when I first moved here I'd be here today, I'd have said you were crazy," he says. I marvel, as I have all year, at their courage, at their decision to choose to live an often unpopular religion. I still can't say whether I would have had the same courage if I hadn't been raised Catholic, but I can say I'm proud to choose it now. This experience with the Works of Mercy has helped me to see how much of my faith must be a choice, how easy it is to become complacent, the need to remind myself to respond to the call of my faith each day. There are so many ways to say yes. Mercy is not something we bestow upon one another from on high in a sort of grand gesture, but rather something much quieter, more humble. It is an invitation, an openness, a kind of accompanying. To have mercy is to give mercy. And to give mercy is to empty oneself out to make room for the love for another.

We round the corner and are some of the first to arrive at the parish center, this room where we've spent so much time together—although now we're joined by a number of other candidates, who've gone through a separate RCIA program. Lauren puts on her robe and Zubair does, as well. I feel a bit like I did when I was the maid of honor at my friend's wedding. Lauren and I stop by the bathroom, and here, so as to avoid a show, I give Lauren her necklace. She says she loves it and puts it on. She seems so confident that what she is about to do is right. "This was all so necessary," she says to me. "It's no longer about wondering what's in front of me. It's that what's in front of me has no limits."

Fr. Collins gathers the group for instruction and guides us step-by-step through what we can expect of the vigil. He warns us that the Scripture readings will be long and that there will be seven of them, instead of the three typically heard at Sunday Mass. He suggests that we let our minds wander during the readings, but in a deliberate way. "If you hear something in the reading that moves you, go with it," he says. "As you listen to the story of creation, and you hear about the creation, and you like creepy-crawly things, let your mind drift off to the creepy-crawly things." This earns some laughter.

Fr. Collins then discusses what will happen during the baptism, and he is talking about the Exodus story, about how we will hear about the Red Sea washing away the Egyptians. But he broadens that story for us, telling us that it is not just about the armies, but also about the power of water. And that we should be reminded of that today during the baptism, reminded of what God has done through water. And then he stops. And everyone waits to hear what he has to say next, and I realize he has tears in his eyes, just barely. "Sorry," he says, "this means a lot to me." Seeing him tear up has me close to crying, too, and I look around and I am so amazed by what we are all about to do. We are meant to be like Velcro with our spons-ees, Fr. Collins reminds us. "Wherever they go, you go," he says. "And when in doubt, put your hand on their shoulder. That physical presence is important."

We rush upstairs to the back of the church, which is already dark. A woman dressed in black ushers us forward, warning us that we need to start on time. Then, moments later, one of the candidates asks if there's a bathroom around. I begin to worry, too. We're all nervous. This will last for hours. I look to another sponsor, and ask: "Do you think we have time to use the bathroom?" Her eyes open wide as she looks at the group gathering around the paschal candle and just says, "Wow." I take this as a no. But Lauren and the Girl Who Is Concerned about the Bathroom overhear me. "Do we have time?" Lauren asks. "Run,"

I say. The three of us sprint to the front of the church and into the hallway that leads to the restroom, only to stand waiting by the door as the woman in black slowly catches up with us, unlocks the door to the parish center, and tells us to hurry. "You're going to miss the start," she says encouragingly.

I swear we get back to that hallway in two minutes. Once again we're in front of a locked door; only this time we're locked out of the church. The Girl Who Is Concerned about the Bathroom pulls on the heavy metal knob, but the door won't budge. I run back to the door that leads to the bathrooms; it has locked behind us. Another door seems to lead to a basement, another to a closet, and yet another is an emergency exit. There are five doors in this hallway, and all of them are locked. The Girl Who Is Concerned about the Bathroom now, loudly, becomes the Girl Who Is Concerned about the Door. She pulls with all her might and then leans back exasperated and loudly expresses what we are all feeling: "You've got to be F——G kidding me!"

"I have worked too hard to miss this," Lauren says with a degree of panic I am beginning to feel but trying not to show. I knew it was my job to help Lauren enter fully into the church; I just didn't expect to do so in such a literal fashion. She runs down some steps toward the emergency exit, and she moves dangerously close to it. I, like a good sponsor, put my hand on her shoulder. "Wait!" I try to say calmly, envisioning the NYFD storming the church and extinguishing the paschal candle in a torrent of water.

We begin banging on the door. "Hello?" I say as quietly as possible while still trying to be heard. "Help us?" The Girl Who Is Concerned about the Door smashes her hand against it with greater force. We all look at one another. I bang loudly. Everything that we have been waiting for is on the other side of that door, so close and yet so very far away. And for a moment, the whole thing is sort of hilarious and tragic all at once: how often I've felt this way, on the edge of the church;

inside, yet not quite there, hoping to be let in more fully, trying with all my might to be heard, to not cause too much trouble, to be a part of this thing that I love that is so beautiful and familiar. "Knock, and the door will be opened for you," Christ told his disciples. But he didn't say how long that would take.

After what seemed like hours, but was likely six minutes, the woman in black opened the door from the other side. Her face conveyed an unmistakable (and understandable) annoyance. Lauren and the Concerned Girl ran by her, their heels clicking on the stone floor toward the back of the church as they rushed inside, toward the light. I followed, all of us quickly moving out of her range.

Moments later we are reunited with the group at the back of the church. We are handed candles, and we take a moment to catch our breath. Despite the calm surroundings, I'm upset. The woman with the keys knew we were back there. How could this have happened? I put my hand on Lauren's shoulder again as we watch the paschal candle slowly being carried up the aisle. Lauren and I fall into line behind the others and walk to the front pews, side by side. Others begin to follow us, although the whole group seems to doubt whether or not we're meant to go up this aisle. But each of us makes it, all at different paces, up the center aisle. It's not necessarily how it's supposed to be, but it seems to represent well how we got here, each in our own time, at our own pace, finally gathering together at the front of the church.

Before Mass begins, the lights of the church are turned off and the space is bathed in darkness. Then, as the liturgy starts, the entire congregation is given small candles, which are slowly lit. This is my favorite part of the Easter Vigil, the Mass that begins the Easter season and celebrates the Resurrection. I remember being an altar server at this Mass at my home parish and seeing this scene from the front of the church. I loved standing up and staring out at the tiny lights that together made the church warmer and brighter. I remember how beautiful it all was, how many familiar faces were illuminated, how happy my parents always looked, seeing me and my siblings on the altar. And then, as the Exsultet begins, I am homesick for a moment.

My mind is filled with vigils of the past: the hours of rehearsals, the reverent carrying of bricks of incense placed onto hot coals, the careful disposal of these same coals in the gutter outside, the wondering if this was OK, and priests warning us not to set off the smoke alarms. I remember the sacristans—volunteers who worked behind the scenes as kind of stage managers for the Mass, and who always smiled at us and urged us on. I remember that one year one of the younger altar boys began picking wax off his candle and eating it. There was the year when I was put in charge of carrying the nails that are symbolically placed in the paschal candle at the start of Mass. Somehow I managed to bring only four of the five needed, and the priest had to mime adding the final one.

Suddenly now, I miss the years when the choir at my hometown parish played the tambourine during a particularly festive song rejoicing about the Pharaoh's army and his chariots being cast into the sea and drowning horrible deaths (Book of Exodus). And I miss catching my sister's eye and trying not to break into laughter every time the song begins. I miss watching as my brother molds his candle into some sort of abstract sculpture or figure throughout the readings. I remember the year when a lector, in the middle of singing the Exsultet, perhaps overcome by the incense, passed out, falling to the floor with a thud. And I miss sitting next to my siblings and my parents, all of us together, faces lit like windows, shining.

"This is the night," says the Exsultet, over and over. When sin is destroyed, people are saved, forgiven, raised up. As I hear the words, I can feel the stress of being locked out of the church gradually leaving me. In place of my worry, even my homesickness, I feel peace. I settle in and I let my mind wander, in a deliberate way, along with the readings, as Fr. Collins suggested. And before I know it, the presider is calling for the presentation of the candidates for baptism.

At the back of the church, volunteers stand around the large stone pool with water flowing down into it from the font. The floor is a mosaic of tiles and gold stars. The volunteers hold ribbons as a kind of barrier meant to create a space in which the RCIA participants can stand.

As we walk toward the font, the choir sings the Litany of the Saints. This is something I've always loved, imagining each saint in his or her time as the name is called. But tonight, it sounds less like a list of people who are dead and gone and more like a roll call of people who are here, alive, and with me tonight. *St. Dominic and St. Francis, pray for us.* I think of the Dominicans who taught me in college. I think of my brother, whose birthday falls on St. Francis's feast. *St. Ignatius, pray for us.* I think of my fellow editors at my office. Of how blessed I am to have the chance, through them, to learn so much more about the kind of spiritual life this saint envisioned. *St. Catherine of Siena, pray for us.* I think of the smart, wonderful women I know who struggle with their relationship with the church. More than ever, I view these saints as so much more than names on a list, more than figures above us; I see them as people whose actions have directly affected my life. In many ways it is because of them that I am here beside so many others who also have followed in the footsteps of holy men and women. All of us together form this great cloud of witnesses.

Jackie is called forward and steps into the pool. She is calm, her lithe figure dressed in black. Her dark, straight hair is pulled back, and she closes her eyes. She has gone through so much to be here: three starts in RCIA, visits to her father in Taiwan, business trips that take her around the world. And as the presider lifts a huge pitcher of water over her head, I wonder for a minute if maybe Jackie will laugh or if she will flinch. I wonder what I would do if I were in her place.

But she simply keeps her face still, and her expression is one of peace and close to noble. She seems so sure. The presider pours two more pitchers. This action—dumping several liters of water over someone's head in the middle of New York City—will be repeated fifteen more times that night at St. Paul's. And it is being repeated countless times that night, all over the city, the country, the world. It seems so absurd and so miraculous; I can barely find the words, until the choir, which has reassembled by the font, sings, "Alleluia!" And Jackie smiles and is wrapped in white. And when the others finish, the rest of us, together, renew our baptismal promises. I look around at the hope in the faces of those beside me. I also remember the problems and the scandal the church continues to face, but I see the love and the hope and Christ personified in others, and it is because of these things, I say, and truly feel, "I do believe."

Afterward, we transition back to our seats, waiting for the newly baptized to change their clothes. The candidates head to the altar, and Zubair and another candidate, who have been baptized as Christians in other denominations, are meant to profess a belief in the Catholic Church. They stand on the altar, and we all stand in a row, all sort of squished together on the altar again, just like before when we were lined up at the Call to Continuing Conversion at St. Patrick's.

The presider looks at Zubair and his fellow candidate. "Please profess your faith in the Catholic Church," he says. They stare at him. The presider nods and smiles. They continue to stare. "I profess?" Zubair tries, looking perplexed. The presider looks equally confused. I am slowly realizing that somehow, somewhere, there was a miscommunication. The text they were meant to read is not there. We look around at one another. The presider looks around and then back at the candidates. All in one breath he says: "Do you profess to the Catholic Church? Yes? OK?" And then he hugs them. And I think: what on earth just happened? And then I think: Welcome. Welcome to our huge, crazy, dysfunctional family. You might as well know now, this is how it's going to be. It's not perfect. Sometimes the church doesn't tell you enough. Sometimes it seems to say too much. And sometimes there are literally no words at all. But we muddle through it together.

The newly baptized return up the center aisle in their white robes, and the crowd on the altar grows. We stretch out the line, and Lauren and I end up at the end. I can see her boyfriend, Brett, taking photos from the pews. She's smiling, and my hand is back on her shoulder, and it's all I can do to keep from hugging her. At my own confirmation, the bishop made a small cross on my forehead with oil, but the presider seems to be taking a different approach. He covers his hand in the oil and smears it across each person's face and then makes a cross with his thumb. The fragrant smell of the oil fills the air.

He finally reaches Lauren, and she looks composed throughout her anointing. As the presider steps away, I smile at her and throw my arm around her shoulder. "Welcome, Thérèse," I say. She laughs and looks out into the crowd to Brett and smiles. I look across the line, and the others are beaming as well, everyone facing forward together, faces shining, new.

EPILOGUE

—IN WHICH I END AND BEGIN
MY JOURNEY IN MERCY

On a warm day in May I walk with my family from the subway through the bright streets and into the rose garden of the old motherhouse of the Sisters of Mercy in Brooklyn. I am not sure what one is meant to wear to a covenant signing, but I have decided on a navy blue sundress with tiny white polka dots. Sisters of Mercy, Mercy Associates, and young Mercy Volunteers slowly filter into the beautiful old chapel, as sunbeams anoint the intricately tiled floor with light. I am there to officially join the Mercy Associates by signing a covenant, which sounds scary but is a yearly commitment. Though it is several weeks behind me now, my Lenten experience of the Corporal Works of Mercy has given extra weight to this moment.

It is, in some ways, an unlikely step for these times, when spiritual-but-not-religious is often the more popular way to go. Instead, I find myself making a formal, public commitment to a particular way of living out an ancient faith. It is also a path that I have found liberating, one that has offered me the freedom to explore. One that reminds me to behave more deliberately when, to use my friend's phrasing, more fully committing to do things I'm supposed to do anyway.

I stand in the center of the chapel beside one other new associate. Aloud, with clear voices, the sisters pledge to support me; these women are promising to be there for me to encourage and advise me. Because it's easy to say, "Who am I in this church? In this world? I am not wanted. I am not worthy." Staying is not easy sometimes. But I believe that the church is more than the sum of its sins. And it is a church in which neither the pope nor the poor are irrelevant. When at our best, we do not write people off. We challenge. We encourage. We love. Sadly, we are not always at our best. But together, we become better.

Joining the Mercy Associates provides me with a community within the larger Catholic community. This decision ultimately has been my own. And yet being a Mercy Associate is not just a way to hole up in my own little corner of the church. It's about becoming better prepared to face the parts that give me pause, the injustices within, about engaging with the larger church and society, feeling renewed and supported.

Sr. Camille once offered me some advice, which was once given to her: "Never let a woman stand alone." But the statement applies to all, men and women alike. This, in some ways, sums up the purpose of living a life of mercy—to let one another know that no one has to go it alone. To provide a place where people will accept you, even with your flaws—and even when your choice of shoes is really, really strange. Standing in the center of that chapel in Brooklyn, in the midst of sisters, associates, coworkers, and friends, the whole group lifts hands in blessing. It's nice to know that, on those days when I doubt, if I'm ever in need, I can grab hold of any one.

After the ceremony, I walk toward the function room, where we share fruit platters and cookies and even a cake brought by my coworkers. In some ways the whole experience felt new, yet it also felt familiar and like I already belonged. And as I chewed on a cookie, I looked around at this bunch of people, some of whom I'd known my whole life and some of whom I'd only recently met. I looked forward to continuing our shared journey on the path of mercy, to places we'd never been, and to the works ahead—works for which none of us is ever quite prepared, but to which all of us are called.

ACKNOWLEDGMENTS

Many, many thanks . . .

To the men and women who serve in and are served by the many ministries of mercy in which I was privileged to participate.

To James Martin, SJ, for his continued patience, reassurance, inspiration, guidance, and subtitle-writing genius. And to Kevin Clarke, for connecting me with his friends back in Chicago.

To Joe Durepos, Vinita Hampton Wright, Andrew Yankech, Steve Connor, Becca Russo, Ray Ives, Rosemary Lane, Yvonne Micheletti, and the entire Loyola Press family who helped to make this book happen. And for making the process enjoyable.

To Lauren Redding, Zubair Simonson, Jackie King, Winnie Morello, and Lisa Harrelson, who made Lent especially meaningful through their insights into faith and conversion. And for allowing me to write about our shared experience.

To Robert Collins, SJ, for his many, many wise and hilarious words of encouragement. And for teaching me so much about what it means to be Catholic, often without any words at all.

To my dear friends, who listened to me say, "I need to finish writing my book," for far, far too long, and never once threatened to punch me. And especially to George Williams, SJ; Paul Rogers; Camille D'Arienzo, RSM; Nick Liao; Brianna McPherson; Mirela

Iverac; Anthony SooHoo, SJ; Tim Levine; and Colm Lynch for their immensely helpful suggestions and edits.

To Matt and Elizabeth, the world's greatest siblings, for their good humor and unfailing love, enthusiasm, and support, which began long before this project.

To my loving, wonderful parents, John and Peggy, who helped me form my faith and are my foundation.

ABOUT THE AUTHOR

Kerry Weber is a Mercy Associate and Managing Editor of *America* magazine. She is an alumna of the Mercy Volunteer Corps and of the Columbia University Graduate School of Journalism. She lives in New York City.